The Simplest Path to Wealth

Turn $50,000 into $3.3 million

Arthur V. Prosper

Copyright©2016 by Arthur V. Prosper * A-Team Publishing Group * PO Box 153 * Pinebrook, New Jersey 07058

COPYRIGHT AND TRADEMARK OWNERSHIP

All rights reserved. No part of this publication may be reproduced, stored in a retrieval system or transmitted by any means, electronic, mechanical, photocopying, recording, scanning or otherwise except as permitted under Section 107 or 108 of the 1976 United States Copyright Act, without the prior permission of the author and publisher.

Please be aware that any unauthorized use of the contents contained herein violates copyright laws, trademark laws, the laws of privacy and publicity, and/or other regulations and statutes. All text, images and other materials provided herein are owned by **Arthur V. Prosper** unless otherwise attributed to third parties. None of the content on these materials may be copied, reproduced, distributed, downloaded, displayed, or transmitted in any form without the prior written permission of **Arthur V. Prosper**, the legal copyright owner. However, you may copy, reproduce, distribute, download, display, or transmit the content of the materials for personal, non-commercial use provided that full attribution and citation to **Arthur V. Prosper** is included and the content is not modified, and you retain all copyright and other proprietary notices contained in the content. The permission stated above is automatically rescinded if you breach any of these terms or conditions. If permission is rescinded or denied, you must immediately destroy any downloaded and/or printed content.

FBI Anti-Piracy Warning: The unauthorized reproduction or distribution of a copyrighted work is illegal. Criminal copyright infringement, including infringement without monetary gain, is investigated by the FBI and is punishable by up to five years in federal prison and a fine of $250,000.

PAPERBACK ISBN: 9781976994012
Imprint: Independently published
Cover Design by Kristjan Victorino
Printed in the United States
Printed in the United States
Author's Email Address: arthurvprosper@gmail.com

Copyright©2016 by Arthur V. Prosper

Also by Arthur V. Prosper

The Six Million Dollar Retiree: Your roadmap to a six million dollar retirement nest egg

Stop Paying Your Credit Cards: Obtain Credit Card Debt Forgiveness Vol 1

Debt Forgiveness, Volume 2 When Creditors Decide to Sue

Dynamic Budgeting Techniques: Cut your expenses in half and double your income

How Much Federal Income Tax Will I Pay in 2018? The New Tax Law's winners and losers

Living Rich & Loving It: Your guide to a rich, happy, healthy, simple and balanced life

DISCLAIMER

Notice: The information contained in this book is provided to you "AS IS" and does not constitute legal or financial advice. The advice provided is general advice only and does not take into account your own personal objectives, financial situation or needs. Consult an attorney or a financial professional before acting on any information provided herein. Any companies, enterprises, organizations and products mentioned in this book are for reference only, have no affiliation with the author or publisher and are not specifically endorsed by the author or publisher.

ABOUT THE AUTHOR

Arthur V. Prosper heads the finance department of a privately held manufacturing firm in the great state of New Jersey. Previously, he was the Vice President of Finance of the Kuoni Group and the Accounting Director of Cantel Medical. He was responsible for the financial objectives, retirement and benefit plans, investment goals and capital structures of the companies he worked for.

Arthur V. Prosper is a freelance writer, author and columnist with 30 years of market experience. He writes articles about the markets and finance under the header "DidoSphere, DidoSpin and Vox Populi". He is the author of several published articles in business, politics, sports and entertainment including: How We Got Here, Market Crash of 2008, Housing Bubble, The Obama Recession, Bank Stress Tests & Other Terms, Scrap Mark to Market Valuation, Recession Over, The Labyrinth of Obamacare, Bush-Obama Recession, No Different From the Rest, A Tale of Two States, NJ & VA, SEC's Case vs. GS&CO., Weak, Most Experts Agree, PIIGS: Too Big to Fail, What Causes Stock Market Fluctuations, Sluggish Recovery, Good for Investors, QE2=Printing Money, Stock Market Investors, Fasten Your Seatbelt, No Double Dip Recession, 10% Unemployment Rate, Not Enough to Derail Recovery

****

Visit the author's website: http://Arthur V. Prosper.com/
Author's email address: Arthur V. Prosper@Arthur V. Prosper.com
****

Table of Contents

Introduction……………………………………………………………..7
PART I – Your path to $3.3 million…………………………….9
   If only…I could have been on my yacht today fishing in the Bahamas…………………………………………………………….9
   Bruce Williams' Advice………………………………………11
   "Time" and "Yield" – the two main ingredients…………12
PART II – LET "YIELD" WORK FOR YOU……………………14
   The Rule of 72……………………………………………………14
   How to earn 12% APY (Annual Percentage Yield)………18
   Market timing strategy…………………………………………34
   What is a stock market crash?………………………………39
   What will cause a stock market crash?……………………40
   The Great Recession, No Different From the Rest………43
   Lie #1 – It's impossible to time the market………………47
   Pinpointing the official start of a recession………………48
   Inverted yield curve, a harbinger of gloom and doom…50
   False negative……………………………………………………64
   How to lose 60% in the stock market………………………66
   How I earned more than 50% return on my money in just one year…………………………………………………………70
   Let us review the lesson………………………………………74
PART III – LET "TIME" WORK FOR YOU……………………76
   The KISS Principle and Auto-Pilot Strategy………………76
   Managing My Investment Portfolio – 30 minutes………79
   Isn't There a Better Investment Strategy?…………………81
   Crockpot method of investing…………………………………92
   Lie #2 – Diversification is good………………………………93
   Investment Strategy - Asset Allocation……………………95

Copyright©2016 by Arthur V. Prosper

PART IV – I AM 5 OR 10 YEARS FROM RETIREMENT, IS IT TOO LATE FOR ME?..98

    Retiring within 10 years………. 98

    Retiring within 5 years………. 99

    Lie #3 - Biggest lie of all – You will pay $400k in taxes on your $1 million savings………. 100

    Investing in retirement & required minimum distribution (RMD)………. 102

    Other investments before and during retirement……… 108

    Annuities, what are they?......... 109

The $50,000 question: What if I don't have $50,000? 117

How does the new tax law affect the investment strategies in this book? 120

Conclusion 122

Living Rich & Loving It 123

Excerpt from the book, Living Rich & Loving It: 126

Supplemental Disclaimer 128

Copyright and Trademark Ownership 129

Introduction..........

I want to thank you for purchasing this book. If this book helped you, your positive Amazon review would be much appreciated.

The goal of this book is to present an investment program that is actionable, easy to implement and points the reader towards the simplest path to financial independence in a step by step fashion. The simplest path to wealth is as follows:

- Maximize your contributions to your retirement account.
- Invest your savings as shown under chapter, "INVESTMENT STRATEGY – ASSET ALLOCATION".
- Take your money out of the stock market ONLY when there is an identifiable recession in sight. For signs of a recession, see Chapter, "PINPOINTING THE OFFICIAL START OF A RECESSION".
- Do not go in and out of the market in times of expansions even if there are major corrections of 20 to 30% in the major indices.
- Go back into the market before the start of the bull market that follows a recession. For signs that a recession is ending, see Chapter, "LET US REVIEW THE LESSON".

This book is for you if you are laid back, simple, down to earth and uncomplicated. This book is for you if you want to worry less about money and focus more on the important things in life such as building bridges, curing diseases, making music, working for world peace, caring for the environment, helping the elderly and disabled, playing with your children and grandchildren, preparing a good meal, watching TV and gardening. There is more to life than money so if you like doing things the easy way, do not like stress and prefer the path of least resistance, this book is for you. You should not spend a big chunk of your life struggling to figure out the best and safest investments. Turning $50,000 into $3.3 million should be as easy as reading this book---and it is.

"Money isn't important until you need it… "
- Grant Cardone

PART I – Your path to $3.3 million……….

If only…I could have been on my yacht today fishing in the Bahamas……….

At age 30, most of us know very little about money. Even those who graduated with a finance or accounting degree will encounter difficulties in putting the theories they learned in college into practice when they get to the real world. If I knew then what I know now, I could have retired at 55 and could have been spending my days on my yacht fishing in the Bahamas and drinking fine wine in the evenings. The problem when we are young is that we are too skeptical to listen to good advice due to many years of indoctrination. We have been listening too long to quips such as, "If something sounds too good to be true, it probably is".

The decade of the eighties was a period when I tuned out to music-radio and tuned in to talk-radio. I took in a lot of talk radio, close to 12 hours a day. I know very little about 80s music but I learned a lot about politics, sports, sex and money from radio personalities who flaunted their knowledge in their respective areas of expertise. I kept a small radio next to my early version PC (personal computer) and listened all day long, non-stop to various talk show programs, switching back and forth to NYC stations, WABC, WNBC, WOR and WMCA while laboriously tinkering with budgets, forecasts and analyses on Lotus 123. I slept with the radio on much to my wife's chagrin, even though I was using headphones. I listened to political discussions, travel, sex, sports, real estate and finance. Most of the programs were "call in" shows meaning listeners called in to voice their opinions, challenge the host or ask for advice. Although I was amused with Dr. Joy Browne's sex advice and

Bob Grant's ultra-conservative antics, the ones I enjoyed the most and found most useful were the financial advice shows of Bruce Williams, Bob Brinker and Bernard Meltzer. Come to think of it, I never called into any of those shows, but many of the callers' problems mirrored my own, so I implemented many of the solutions the hosts propounded. I learned a lot from those shows but one of my biggest regrets in life is not listening to Bruce Williams' advice.

Bruce Williams' Advice……….

On one of his shows in the early eighties, right after his usual, "Welcome my friends, welcome to my world" intro, Bruce Williams went right into the news of the day. I can remember as if it were yesterday, he said, "In today's financial news, you can now buy a non-callable 30 year T-bond (30 year treasury bond) with a guaranteed interest rate of 14.5%. Imagine my friends, if you invest your $50,000 today you will have $2.5 million in 30 years. You don't have to invest in anything else. You don't have to buy gold, real estate or do anything fancy." I did not follow the advice, not because I did not have the cash (in fact my wife and I had close to $100,000 in the bank by then) but because, 1) 30 years is such a long time and retirement at that age was the furthest thing from my mind, 2) the advice simply sounded too good to be true. It sounded so incredible in its simplicity, it cannot possibly work, so I thought. There must be a catch somewhere. So I cast it off as satire or hyperbole from a talk show host always on the look-out for ratings. How wrong I was!!! Imagine my friends, had I followed this sound advice from a talk show host, with little risk, my $100,000 would have grown to $5 million in 30 years. I could have retired in my fifties, in pursuit of Marlin on my own 40-foot fishing boat off Cabo San Lucas. Instead, I squandered a big chunk of my money pursuing riskier, more exotic investments (See Chapter, *"Isn't There a Better Investment Strategy?)*. Today you will find me still tinkering with budgets, forecasts and analyses, albeit on excel which is faster than Lotus 123, so I have a little extra time to write books which I hope will someday become best sellers.

"Time" and "Yield" – the two main ingredients……….

"Time" and "Yield" are the two main ingredients in Bruce's recipe. Although the element of Time has changed for me since I first heard the advice, Time remains the same, ready to work for those who are the same age I was when I first heard the advice. However, Yield has changed. Gone are the 14.5% Treasury bonds. They are just now relics of bygone days along with The Wonder Years, Growing Pains and Happy Days. But not all is lost. If you follow the advice in this book, Time and Yield will work the same way for you and yield the same result in the same timeline as Bruce predicted. It is really that simple!

Therefore, in almost the same way Bruce said it, I dare say, "Imagine my friends, if you can put aside $50,000 ("principal") at the age of 30, never touch the principal together with the profit that money earns for 37 years, your $50,000 can grow into $3.3 million by the time you reach full retirement age". **You can double your money every six years.** You don't have to add new money to the principal or invest any of the money in other investments such as real estate, commodities, foreign currencies, precious metals and collectibles. You don't have to invest in any business. The trick is you will let "Time" and "Yield" do their job. You will not touch this money and the money it earns…if you can help it. This will be your "Security Fund" ("SF") NOT your "emergency fund". The extra pot of gold at the end of the rainbow. Think of this money as "no longer yours" stashed away in a lock box, lost and forgotten. Or you might just consider this money "already spent". Lock this money up and forget it. Then all you have to do is sit back and watch this SF grow from $50,000 into $3.3 million. This book will show you how to achieve this goal."

"Fortune sides with him who dares."
- Virgil

PART II – LET "YIELD" WORK FOR YOU..........

The Rule of 72..........

The components need for our investment program to turn $50,000 into $3.3 million are: Time=37 years & Annual Percentage Yield (APY) = 12%. Since Long-term treasuries are no longer earning north of 14%, how can you accomplish this goal in today's economic climate with the Feds' "lower for longer interest rates policy"? You can and will by following the strategy in this book but you will just have to accept the fact that to earn at least 12% APY you will have to invest in equities (the stock market). Even if you are a risk averse investor this book is for you as long as you are willing to follow the system outlined in this book. But you must understand that investing in equities is 100% more risky than investing in treasury bonds, although the strategy should minimize the risk.

The Rule of 72 is a quick way to figure out approximately how long your investment will take to double in value if you apply a fixed interest rate with annual compounding. The formula is 72/APY = the number of years it will take for your investment to double. Conversely, to find out the APY you will have to earn for your investment to double in 6 years, the formula is: 72/6 = 12% APY which is the average APY you will need to hit our target of $3.3 million in 37 years. The growth of a $50,000 investment at 12% APY for 36 years using the Rule of 72 is shown below:

RULE OF 72	
AGE	HOW MONEY DOUBLES
30	$50,000
36	$100,000
42	$200,000
48	$400,000
54	$800,000
60	$1,600,000
66	$3,200,000

A more detailed computation of the annual growth of a $50,000 investment earning 12% APY for 37 years is shown on the following chart:

How your $50,000 savings will grow by the time you are 67 years old:

Age	Starting Amount	Interest (12%)	Ending Amount
31	50,000	6,000	56,000
32	56,000	6,720	62,720
33	62,720	7,526	70,246
34	70,246	8,430	78,676
35	78,676	9,441	88,117
36	88,117	10,574	98,691
37	98,691	11,843	110,534
38	110,534	13,264	123,798
39	123,798	14,856	138,654
40	138,654	16,638	155,292
41	155,292	18,635	173,927
42	173,927	20,871	194,799
43	194,799	23,376	218,175
44	218,175	26,181	244,356
45	244,356	29,323	273,678
46	273,678	32,841	306,520
47	306,520	36,782	343,302
48	343,302	41,196	384,498
49	384,498	46,140	430,638
50	430,638	51,677	482,315
51	482,315	57,878	540,192
52	540,192	64,823	605,016
53	605,016	72,602	677,617
54	677,617	81,314	758,931
55	758,931	91,072	850,003
56	850,003	102,000	952,004
57	952,004	114,240	1,066,244
58	1,066,244	127,949	1,194,193
59	1,194,193	143,303	1,337,497
60	1,337,497	160,500	1,497,996
61	1,497,996	179,760	1,677,756
62	1,677,756	201,331	1,879,086
63	1,879,086	225,490	2,104,577
64	2,104,577	252,549	2,357,126
65	2,357,126	282,855	2,639,981
66	2,639,981	316,798	2,956,779
67	2,956,779	354,813	3,311,592
INTEREST EARNED		$3,261,592	

The next chart proves the power of time and compounding. If this principal only has 24 years to grow instead of 37 years, (i.e. you locked away your SF at the age of 43) the principal will only grow to $800,000 instead of $3.3 million.

AGE	HOW MONEY DOUBLES
43	50,000
49	100,000
55	200,000
61	400,000
67	800,000

It's incredible that a mere 12-year delay will result in such a big difference in the ending balance.

How to earn 12% APY (Annual Percentage Yield)……….

Now that we have defined our goal, we need a roadmap for the implementation and execution of the game plan to take you from here to there. All we need is a strategy to earn an APY of 12%. If you fail to follow the stock market timing strategy in the following chapters, the $50,000 you will put into the lock box may not earn 12% APY. The simplest, most efficient and least stressful way to invest in the stock market is by putting your investment into mutual funds inside your qualified retirement plan. The most popular qualified retirement plans are: IRA, 401k, 403b, 457b, Roth IRA and Roth 401k.

A detailed analysis to help you choose whether to put your retirement savings into a **traditional IRA/401k or Roth IRA/401k** is shown in the book, *"The Six Million Dollar Retiree" ("6m$Retiree").*

https://www.amazon.com/Six-Million-Dollar-Retiree-retirement-ebook/dp/B073XTL47J/ref=pd_sim_351_6?_encoding=UTF8&psc=1&refRID=BS5AVD0TE1AV80PCTDEC

Individual stock picking, buying corporate stocks and bonds is more complicated and will create more stress in your life. If you have more than $50,000 in your retirement account you may designate $50,000 of your balance and consider it your SF. The way this can be accomplished is by putting $50,000 into one or two mutual funds with solid and proven records of long-term yield of at least 12% APY and which are not likely to fall by the wayside in this lifetime. See the following examples:

Oldest Mutual Funds by Inception Date (Still Active)

Rank	Name	Date of Creation
1	MFS Massachusetts Investors Fund (MITTX)	1924
2	Putnam Investors Fund (PINVX)	1925
3	Pioneer Fund (PIODX)	1928
4	Century Shares Fund (CENSX)	1928
5	Vanguard Wellington Fund (VWELX)	1929
7	CGM Mutual Fund (LOMMX)	1929
6	Seligman Common Stock Fund (SCSFX)	1930
8	Fidelity Fund (FFIDX)	1930
9	Dodge & Cox Balance Fund (DODBX)	1931

Read more: What are the oldest mutual funds, by date of inception?
http://www.investopedia.com/ask/answers/08/oldestmutualfunds.asp#ixzz4tKAoWyPK
http://news.morningstar.com/fund-category-returns/

The aforementioned mutual funds are given as examples only. The management of a particular fund and its current performance may be drastically different from the time of publication of this book. Do your due diligence before acting on any information obtained from this book. For starters, Morningstar and U.S. News and World Report are good websites to check out the attributes and qualities of various funds.

Example of partitioning your traditional or Roth IRA or 401k account balance is as follows:

IRA/401k Balance = $75,000

Security Fund (SF) = $25,000 Century Shares Fund (CENSX)

Security Fund (SF) = $25,000 Pioneer Fund (PIODX)

Balance (Pot of Gold (POG)) = $25,000 invested in other funds

In the above scenario, leave your SF alone for 37 years and it should grow into $3.3 million. Continue filling up your POG as much as possible although you really do not have to add to it. However, there is an enormous advantage in deferring a big portion of your earned income from taxation as part of retirement planning as discussed in greater detail in the book, *"The Six Million Dollar Retiree" ("6m$Retiree").*

If CENSX and PIODX are not available in your Plan's list of mutual funds, and none of the nine oldest funds as shown on the preceding chart of Oldest Mutual Funds is available, ask your benefits administrator which one of the available funds is the oldest and had the highest average earnings from inception date.

According to historical data, the average annualized return of the S&P 500 index, not inflation adjusted, since 1928 was 11.42% as shown on the following chart:

S&P 500 INDEX
HISTORICAL RETURNS
(SOURCE:

https://ycharts.com/indicators/sandp_500_total_return_annual
)

YEAR	ANNUALIZED YIELD
1928	43.81%
1929	-8.30%
1930	-25.12%
1931	-43.84%
1932	-8.64%
1933	49.98%
1934	-1.19%
1935	46.74%
1936	31.94%
1937	-35.34%
1938	29.28%
1939	-1.10%
1940	-10.67%
1941	-12.77%
1942	19.17%
1943	25.06%
1944	19.03%
1945	35.82%
1946	-8.43%

Year	Return
1947	5.20%
1948	5.70%
1949	18.30%
1950	30.81%
1951	23.68%
1952	18.15%
1953	-1.21%
1954	52.56%
1955	32.60%
1956	7.44%
1957	-10.46%
1958	43.72%
1959	12.06%
1960	0.34%
1961	26.64%
1962	-8.81%
1963	22.61%
1964	16.42%
1965	12.40%
1966	-9.97%
1967	23.80%
1968	10.81%
1969	-8.24%
1970	3.56%
1971	14.22%
1972	18.76%
1973	-14.31%
1974	-25.90%
1975	37.00%
1976	23.83%
1977	-6.98%
1978	6.51%

Year	Return
1979	18.52%
1980	31.74%
1981	-4.70%
1982	20.42%
1983	22.34%
1984	6.15%
1985	31.24%
1986	18.49%
1987	5.81%
1988	16.54%
1989	31.48%
1990	-3.06%
1991	30.23%
1992	7.49%
1993	9.97%
1994	1.33%
1995	37.20%
1996	22.68%
1997	33.10%
1998	28.34%
1999	20.89%
2000	-9.03%
2001	-11.85%
2002	-21.97%
2003	28.36%
2004	10.74%
2005	4.83%
2006	15.61%
2007	5.48%
2008	-36.55%
2009	25.94%
2010	14.82%

2011	2.10%
2012	15.89%
2013	32.15%
2014	13.52%
2015	1.36%
2016	11.96%
	1016.23%
AVERAGE	11.42%

With dividends reinvested the returns were even more, close to 13%. In the past 42 years, some equity and growth mutual funds returned more than an annualized average yield of 13% NOT adjusted for inflation. The effect of inflation may be estimated as a 3% reduction from the gains, but for this discussion and analysis, we will not deduct the inflation rate from the returns. For most people, inflation is of little consequence when the return on investment is in the millions. Review the 4 charts that follow showing the 42-year performance of the 4 oldest mutual funds still in existence today. You will be amazed by how much your mere $50,000 would have grown in 42 years:

CHART 1				
MFS Massachusetts Investors Fund (MITTX)				
Inception Year: 1924				
(Source: https://finance.yahoo.com)				
Year	Annualized Yield	Beginning	Interest	Ending
1975	33.12%	50,000	16,560	66,560
1976	23.63%	66,560	15,728	82,288
1977	-11.06%	82,288	-9,101	73,187
1978	8.28%	73,187	6,060	79,247
1979	21.99%	79,247	17,426	96,673
1980	30.62%	96,673	29,601	126,275
1981	-4.89%	126,275	-6,175	120,100
1982	18.89%	120,100	22,687	142,787
1983	20.89%	142,787	29,828	172,615
1984	2.94%	172,615	5,075	177,690
1985	24.56%	177,690	43,641	221,330
1986	17.21%	221,330	38,091	259,421
1987	7.46%	259,421	19,353	278,774
1988	10.38%	278,774	28,937	307,711
1989	36.12%	307,711	111,145	418,856
1990	-0.10%	418,856	-419	418,437
1991	27.67%	418,437	115,782	534,219
1992	7.38%	534,219	39,425	573,644
1993	10.03%	573,644	57,537	631,181
1994	-1.02%	631,181	-6,438	624,743
1995	39.34%	624,743	245,774	870,517
1996	25.90%	870,517	225,464	1,095,980
1997	31.69%	1,095,980	347,316	1,443,297

Year	%	Start	Change	End
1998	22.95%	1,443,297	331,237	1,774,533
1999	6.96%	1,774,533	123,508	1,898,041
2000	-0.34%	1,898,041	-6,453	1,891,587
2001	-16.24%	1,891,587	-307,194	1,584,394
2002	-22.00%	1,584,394	-348,567	1,235,827
2003	22.14%	1,235,827	273,612	1,509,439
2004	11.51%	1,509,439	173,736	1,683,176
2005	7.29%	1,683,176	122,703	1,805,879
2006	13.20%	1,805,879	238,376	2,044,255
2007	10.61%	2,044,255	216,895	2,261,150
2008	-32.81%	2,261,150	-741,883	1,519,267
2009	27.73%	1,519,267	421,293	1,940,560
2010	11.43%	1,940,560	221,806	2,162,366
2011	-1.83%	2,162,366	-39,571	2,122,794
2012	19.15%	2,122,794	406,515	2,529,310
2013	31.90%	2,529,310	806,850	3,336,159
2014	10.99%	3,336,159	366,644	3,702,803
2015	0.28%	3,702,803	10,368	3,713,171
2016	8.77%	3,713,171	325,645	4,038,816
	512.72%			
Average	12.21%			

CHART 2

Putnam Investors Fund (PINVX)

Inception Year: 1925

(Source: https://finance.yahoo.com)

Year	Annualized Yield	Beginning	Interest	Ending
1975	21.26%	50,000	10,630	60,630
1976	20.39%	60,630	12,362	72,992
1977	-3.18%	72,992	-2,321	70,671
1978	13.90%	70,671	9,823	80,495
1979	20.14%	80,495	16,212	96,706
1980	44.47%	96,706	43,005	139,711
1981	-8.83%	139,711	-12,337	127,375
1982	33.66%	127,375	42,874	170,249
1983	10.75%	170,249	18,302	188,551
1984	0.15%	188,551	283	188,834
1985	29.20%	188,834	55,140	243,974
1986	15.74%	243,974	38,401	282,375
1987	4.00%	282,375	11,295	293,670
1988	7.48%	293,670	21,967	315,636
1989	33.92%	315,636	107,064	422,700
1990	-2.77%	422,700	-11,709	410,992
1991	28.56%	410,992	117,379	528,371
1992	7.89%	528,371	41,688	570,059
1993	17.87%	570,059	101,870	671,929
1994	-3.19%	671,929	-21,435	650,494
1995	37.55%	650,494	244,261	894,755
1996	21.40%	894,755	191,478	1,086,232
1997	34.49%	1,086,232	374,642	1,460,874

Year	%	Start	Change	End
1998	35.52%	1,460,874	518,902	1,979,776
1999	30.14%	1,979,776	596,705	2,576,481
2000	-18.50%	2,576,481	-476,649	2,099,832
2001	-24.80%	2,099,832	-520,758	1,579,074
2002	-23.81%	1,579,074	-375,977	1,203,096
2003	27.62%	1,203,096	332,295	1,535,391
2004	12.76%	1,535,391	195,916	1,731,307
2005	8.81%	1,731,307	152,528	1,883,835
2006	13.89%	1,883,835	261,665	2,145,500
2007	-5.06%	2,145,500	-108,562	2,036,938
2008	-40.29%	2,036,938	-820,682	1,216,256
2009	31.17%	1,216,256	379,107	1,595,363
2010	14.06%	1,595,363	224,308	1,819,670
2011	-0.17%	1,819,670	-3,093	1,816,577
2012	16.56%	1,816,577	300,825	2,117,402
2013	35.04%	2,117,402	741,938	2,859,340
2014	13.77%	2,859,340	393,731	3,253,071
2015	-2.53%	3,253,071	-82,303	3,170,768
2016	12.06%	3,170,768	382,395	3,553,163
	521.09%			
Average	12.41%			

CHART 3				
Pioneer Fund (PIODX)				
Inception Year: 1928				
(Source: https://finance.yahoo.com)				
Year	Annualized Yield	Beginning	Interest	Ending
1975	39.32%	50,000	19,660	69,660
1976	36.86%	69,660	25,677	95,337
1977	3.66%	95,337	3,489	98,826
1978	12.29%	98,826	12,146	110,972
1979	27.88%	110,972	30,939	141,911
1980	30.71%	141,911	43,581	185,491
1981	-3.01%	185,491	-5,583	179,908
1982	13.49%	179,908	24,270	204,178
1983	24.92%	204,178	50,881	255,059
1984	-0.88%	255,059	-2,245	252,814
1985	26.03%	252,814	65,808	318,622
1986	11.49%	318,622	36,610	355,231
1987	4.81%	355,231	17,087	372,318
1988	18.33%	372,318	68,246	440,564
1989	23.39%	440,564	103,048	543,612
1990	-10.49%	543,612	-57,025	486,587
1991	22.75%	486,587	110,699	597,286
1992	13.80%	597,286	82,425	679,711
1993	14.23%	679,711	96,723	776,434
1994	-0.58%	776,434	-4,503	771,931
1995	26.64%	771,931	205,642	977,573
1996	19.70%	977,573	192,582	1,170,155
1997	38.47%	1,170,155	450,158	1,620,313

Year	Return	Start	Change	End
1998	29.09%	1,620,313	471,349	2,091,662
1999	15.54%	2,091,662	325,044	2,416,707
2000	0.12%	2,416,707	2,900	2,419,607
2001	-11.13%	2,419,607	-269,302	2,150,304
2002	-20.26%	2,150,304	-435,652	1,714,653
2003	24.58%	1,714,653	421,462	2,136,114
2004	11.63%	2,136,114	248,430	2,384,544
2005	6.39%	2,384,544	152,372	2,536,917
2006	16.39%	2,536,917	415,801	2,952,718
2007	4.70%	2,952,718	138,778	3,091,495
2008	-34.38%	3,091,495	-1,062,856	2,028,639
2009	24.24%	2,028,639	491,742	2,520,381
2010	15.71%	2,520,381	395,952	2,916,333
2011	-4.58%	2,916,333	-133,568	2,782,765
2012	9.91%	2,782,765	275,772	3,058,537
2013	33.06%	3,058,537	1,011,152	4,069,690
2014	10.87%	4,069,690	442,375	4,512,065
2015	-0.43%	4,512,065	-19,402	4,492,663
2016	9.60%	4,492,663	431,296	4,923,959
	534.86%			
Average	12.73%			

CHART 4			
Century Shares Fund (CENSX)			
Inception Year: 1928			
(Source: https://finance.yahoo.com)			
Year	Annualized Yield	Beginning	Interest	Ending
1975	14.28%	50,000	7,140	57,140
1976	36.77%	57,140	21,010	78,150
1977	-2.11%	78,150	-1,649	76,501
1978	9.91%	76,501	7,581	84,083
1979	21.67%	84,083	18,221	102,303
1980	6.40%	102,303	6,547	108,851
1981	20.18%	108,851	21,966	130,817
1982	11.00%	130,817	14,390	145,207
1983	21.00%	145,207	30,493	175,700
1984	15.48%	175,700	27,198	202,899
1985	43.40%	202,899	88,058	290,957
1986	9.61%	290,957	27,961	318,918
1987	-8.02%	318,918	-25,577	293,340
1988	15.69%	293,340	46,025	339,365
1989	41.64%	339,365	141,312	480,677
1990	-7.84%	480,677	-37,685	442,992
1991	31.51%	442,992	139,587	582,579
1992	26.99%	582,579	157,238	739,817
1993	-0.36%	739,817	-2,663	737,154
1994	-3.90%	737,154	-28,749	708,405
1995	35.23%	708,405	249,571	957,976
1996	17.16%	957,976	164,389	1,122,364
1997	50.13%	1,122,364	562,641	1,685,005

Year	Return	Start	Gain/Loss	End
1998	7.00%	1,685,005	117,950	1,802,956
1999	-12.38%	1,802,956	-223,206	1,579,750
2000	37.44%	1,579,750	591,458	2,171,208
2001	-2.52%	2,171,208	-54,714	2,116,494
2002	-12.57%	2,116,494	-266,043	1,850,451
2003	25.03%	1,850,451	463,168	2,313,618
2004	12.51%	2,313,618	289,434	2,603,052
2005	6.34%	2,603,052	165,033	2,768,086
2006	10.02%	2,768,086	277,362	3,045,448
2007	6.67%	3,045,448	203,131	3,248,579
2008	-36.25%	3,248,579	-1,177,610	2,070,969
2009	27.15%	2,070,969	562,268	2,633,237
2010	14.99%	2,633,237	394,722	3,027,960
2011	0.49%	3,027,960	14,837	3,042,797
2012	13.70%	3,042,797	416,863	3,459,660
2013	32.96%	3,459,660	1,140,304	4,599,964
2014	13.40%	4,599,964	616,395	5,216,359
2015	8.00%	5,216,359	417,309	5,633,667
2016	0.66%	5,633,667	37,182	5,670,850
	558.46%			
Average	13.30%			

The aforementioned mutual funds are not specifically recommended. They are used for illustration purpose only. Do your due diligence whenever choosing an investment.

Notice on Chart No. 4 that if you invested your $50,000 in the Century fund and just left your money alone for 42 years, your $50,000 would have grown to $5.67 million. Also notice in the same chart that in the year 2008, you would have lost $1.18 million because of the stock market crash that happened in the last quarter of 2008. Without that loss, the ending balance of this portfolio would have been at least $6.9 million. That is an incredible growth of a mere $50,000.

Part of our strategy outlined in this book is to get out of the stock market, i.e. stock mutual funds, bond funds and individual stocks before the crash to avoid the devaluation of your investment. Stocks typically lose 30% to 60% of their value during the bear market that follows recessions. A simplified timing strategy to avoid catastrophic losses is an integral part of our game plan. See Chapter, ***"Lie #1 – It's Impossible to Time the Market"***.

If you follow this timing strategy you will minimize your losses or may not lose anything at all when the market crashes. Following this timing strategy, I got out of my mutual funds in August 2007 and got back into stocks only in December 2008. So I lost nothing in 2008 and gained almost 50% in 2009. I define a stock market crash as a 30-60% (or higher) decline in the stock market major indices, DJIA, S&P 500 and NASDAQ which usually signifies that we are in the middle of a recession. I do not consider a decline of under 30% a crash but a correction. Corrections will happen periodically in periods of economic expansions.

> *"Money is only a tool. It will take you wherever you wish, but it will not replace you as the driver."*
> *— Ayn Rand, Atlas Shrugged*

Market timing strategy..........

The market timing strategy outlined in this book will always outperform the "buy, hold and stay the course" strategy which most financial planners, stock market experts, best-selling personal finance authors and investment gurus espouse. Most financial advisors can give investors competent advice on what stocks to buy but most of them do not have an exit strategy to avoid catastrophic losses when the stock market crashes. They say, "Buy, hold and stay the course because stocks eventually recover and always soar to new highs after the crash". But isn't it better to get out of the stock market before the bust and get back in before the boom?

The timing strategy offered in this book is to strive to hit the bullseye twice, i.e. 1) to get out of stocks before the start of the next bear market that follows a recession so as to avoid the typical 30-60% loss of value of stocks and, 2) to get back into stocks close to the bottom of that bear market. **This is a mantra that will be repeated several times in this book to reinforce this technique.** We learn through repetition and repetition may provide a sense of urgency to persuade readers that it is critical to memorize and follow this system so as to avoid a huge devaluation of their portfolio when the crash comes. If you have a tax deferred retirement plan, an IRA, a 401k, 403b or 457b and your money is invested in the stock market, are you prepared to lose as much as 60% of your money when the market crashes? It is not a question of "if" but "when". It is guaranteed the stock market will crash when the next recession arrives, but when will that be?

How come doomsayers never get the timing right? In March 2016, billionaire Carl Icahn raised a red flag on a national broadcast when he declared, *"The public is walking into a trap again as they did in 2007"*. Prophetic economist Andrew Smithers warns, *"U.S. stocks are now 80% overvalued"*.

In his Op-Ed of February 2016, Paul B. Farrell of marketwatch.com forecasts at least a 50% stock market crash and adds, *"But the crash of 2016 really is coming. Dead ahead. Maybe not till we get a bit closer to the presidential election cycle of 2016. But a crash is a sure bet, it's guaranteed certain: Complete with echoes of the 2008 crash, which impacted on the GOP election results, triggering a $10 trillion loss of market cap ... like the 1999 dot-com collapse, it's post-millennium loss of $8 trillion market cap, plus a 30-month recession ... moreover a lot like the 1929 crash and the long depression that followed".* This is a chilling commentary from a respected economist, market expert and columnist of Market Watch, but his prediction did not come true. He finally said, *"So finally I gave up on timing the market---all I know now is that the market truly is random and unpredictable. In fact, only a damn fool would try to outguess it. Flow with it, maybe".* Paul B. Farrell is gracious enough to admit that he does not know anything about market timing.

In his book "The Age of Deception", **James Dale Davidson** predicted a "Black Swan" event with the stock market plunging more than 50% and with the Dow Jones Industrial Averages (DJIA or DOW) dropping 80% in 2016. He promises to tell you what to do to protect your investments and how to "survive and prosper" through the stock market crash that he is certain is coming in 2016. A drop in the Dow of 80% can only mean that he is forecasting a severe recession or worse, a depression in 2016. ***UPDATE***Towards the end of 2016, when it became clear that his prediction of a market crash in 2016 was not going to happen, James Dale Davidson changed his tune and now predicts the economic crash to happen in 2017. He says our economy is like a sandcastle and cracks are forming at the very base. Our entire country rests on an unstable foundation. *"As you can see, all it will take is one grain of sand ... just one ... to send everything crashing. In the end, we will* *see the stock market tumble by 50% ... real estate will plummet by 40% ... savings accounts will lose 30%, and unemployment will triple"*, he continues.

I disagree and here is why: The economy continues to be sluggish and many economists think we are in a secular stagnation. We are following a "lower interest rates longer policy". Fed Chair Janet Yellen's 25 basis points (.25%) announced benchmark federal funds rate increase scheduled for June 2016 (projected 1.4% total for 2016) should not cause an inverted yield curve (a.k.a. negative yield curved) which is one of the best predictors of an impending recession. The increase may not even happen if leading economic indicators such as GDP and private payroll employment remain stagnant. Copper prices have been holding steady at over $2 per pound. If Copper prices go below $2 per pound and stay there for a couple of months, then I will start worrying. Capacity utilization which is a measure of the output of existing factories for manufacturing, utilities (electric and gas), mining, durable goods and non-durable goods has not been dropping. We are 7 years into this bull market and many financial pundits think that U.S. stocks are overvalued. But I still do not believe there will be a recession in 2017 or 2018. James Dale Davidson is selling his book along with his newsletter subscription for more than $200. Just in case you are sold on his gloom and doom scenario that the Dow will drop 80% in 2017 or 2018, get your money out of equities right now and put your entire portfolio in a money market fund. You will not lose money if the Dow drops 80%. Wait for the crash, then buy back the stocks when their value drop 50%. Why buy his $200 book? In my case I am not convinced that a recession is coming in 2017 or 2018 so I want my money to make a little bit more money before the bust. When will that be? See the timeline under chapter, **"Inverted Yield Curve, a Harbinger of Gloom and Doom"**.

My financial advisor lost 60% of her savings in the stock market crash of 2008 (see the chapter **"How to Lose 60% in the Stock Market"**). I lost nothing by following a reliable stock market timing system. The chart in Chapter, **"Inverted Yield Curve..."** shows a timeline as to when to get out of equities and when to get back in. I got out of equities a year before the crash and avoided a 40% devaluation of my portfolio. Then my portfolio gained more than 50% in 2009. The Federal Reserve Bank of St. Louis reported that household wealth plunged $16 trillion from the beginning of the last recession until it ended in June 2009. As of mid-2013, my financial advisor had not yet recovered all the money she lost. If you succeed in following the strategy in this book, you will never lose money in the stock market. In fact you could make a killing when the next recession hits just by following my stress-free KISS strategy which is explained further under the chapter, **"How I Earned More Than 50% in Just One Year"**. The following two charts are examples of how I was positioned when the yield curve inverted. A more detailed explanation of these charts is in the same chapter:

Mutual Fund 1			PPS		Shares	Total
Jul	17	2006	$ 52	INVERSION		
Jul	17	2007	$ 61	ANNIVERSARY OF INVERSION		
Aug	13	2007	$ 58	GOT OUT OF STOCKS	5,000	290,000.00
Dec	01	2008	$ 30	NBER DECLARED RECESSION STARTED DEC 2007		
Dec	02	2008	$ 31	GOT BACK INTO STOCKS	9,355	290,000.00
Dec	30	2009	$ 50	BALANCE IN THIS FUND AS OF THIS DATE	9,355	467,750.00
				$ INCREASE IN VALUE		$ 177,750.00
				% INCREASE IN VALUE		61.3%

Mutual Fund 2	PPS		Shares	Total
Jul 17, 2006	$36	INVERSION		
Jul 17, 2007	$44	ANNIVERSARY OF INVERSION		
Aug 13, 2007	$40	GOT OUT OF STOCKS	5,000	200,000.00
Dec 01, 2008	$20	NBER DECLARED RECESSION STARTED DEC 2007		
Dec 02, 2008	$21	GOT BACK INTO STOCKS	9,524	200,004.00
Dec 30, 2009	$30	BALANCE IN THIS FUND AS OF THIS DATE	9,524	285,720.00
		$ INCREASE IN VALUE		$ 85,720.00
		% INCREASE IN VALUE		42.9%

What is a stock market crash?..........

I define stock market crash as a 30-60% (or higher) decline in the stock market major indices, DJIA, S&P 500 and NASDAQ. I do not consider a decline of under 30% a crash but a correction. Corrections will happen periodically in periods of economic expansions. More than 30% decline in these market indices usually signifies that we are in a bear market in the middle of a U.S. recession. The stock market will crash, but when? The answer is when the economy goes into a recession. It is the goal of this book to guide stock market investors how to look for signs of a recession so that they may exit the market before the start of the bear market that follows and get back in close to the bottom of that bear market.

What will cause a stock market crash?..........

Ken Little who authored 12 books on investing and personal finance gives the following reasons for stock market crashes: Interest rates, inflation, earnings, oil and energy prices, war and terrorism, crime and fraud and serious domestic political unrest. With all due respect to Mr. Little, what he pointed out are the symptoms of the disease rather than the disease itself. The disease which causes the stock market to crash is recession. The stock market will fall and may turn bearish at the onset of various bad news such as an increase in interest rates and sudden increase or decrease in energy prices, instability of the Euro Banking system and the high jobless rate. But if these factors do not lead to a recession, the stock market should quickly recover from a bear market and continue to rise. Sudden market fluctuation is significant for short-term traders but should not be for long term investors. The market always recovers even after a recession and always soars to new highs during periods of expansions. It would be great if you can predict the highs and lows of the market. You could have made a killing if you had sold in October 2007 when the Dow hit 14,000 and bought your stocks back in March 2009 when it plunged to a low of 6,600. The Eurozone problem, high jobless rate, Syrian war, terrorism, conflict in the South China sea, North Korea and Iran do not worry me as much when it comes to my investments as decrease in retail sales, reduction in hiring, declining commodity prices, industrial production and housing starts. The day-traders may drive down the stock market purely on investor sentiment and the major stock market indices may go down by 20% in just a few days, but it defies logic for a downward trend to continue if all leading economic indicators are pointing upwards to...no recession. This is all intricately connected. If stocks do not recover quickly after a 20% correction and we get into a prolonged bear market, consumer confidence may erode resulting in reduced consumer spending which can then lead to a recession. There should not be a protracted bear market unless we are heading into another recession. If you try to time the market during the boom cycle of the economy you will surely lose. Buying and selling during short term peaks and lows in the stock market in times of expansion is for professional traders who do it for a living. For us ordinary investors, we would be better off to leave our IRA and 401k savings accounts alone, invested in mutual funds until an identifiable recession is in sight. We cannot possibly beat traders and professional analysts who lived and breathed this stuff every day, all day long. We must go back to basics to enable us to assess where we are now in the economic recovery. As of this writing in 2016, we are 7 years into this recovery. The great recession ended in June 2009. The great recession was not followed by a great recovery. The economy is sluggish. GDP has been hovering around 2-3% per annum. Interest rates are low and will remain low for the foreseeable future. There is no sign of a recession at the time of writing.

  Stock market crashes are feared by all stock market investors. They result in the sudden reduction of wealth. If you need to get to your money after your portfolio lost 50% of its value, your paper losses will turn into real losses. If you get out of equities after they have lost 50% of their value because you think their value might drop some more, you will lock in your losses. You will not know when to get back in. The timing strategy outlined in this book should serve as a guide. Leave your money alone during boom times, take your money out of stocks ONLY before the beginning of the bear market that follows a recession. Recessions are merely temporary suspension of consumer spending so we can be sure that economic growth will follow recessions. Recessions may become prolonged due to some event that may cause a bank run or collapse of the banking system, another bubble burst or some kind of a natural disaster. Reduction of income; job insecurity; debt increase due to higher interest rates; inflation; diminution of assets, of investments and other tangible property such as real estate will prolong a recession.

The Great Recession, No Different From the Rest..........

It is important to review my published article below to get a clearer picture of my investment philosophy and why I believe the "KISS Principle" of investing and my stress-free "Auto-Pilot" investment strategy are the best and simplest strategies to follow. Investing is not rocket-science. It should be simple and stress-free. Investing should not keep you awake at night worrying about how your investments would do tomorrow.

****

BY Arthur V. Prosper, OCT 18, 2009

Many economists, prognosticators, financial pundits, stock brokers and financial planners have committed a big blunder or a big hoax by proclaiming this recession different from the rest and the worst since the great depression. The fact is I believe this recession is no different from the previous post war recessions. Those who share my belief have made a lot of money in the stock market. In the first quarter of this year, the majority of financial pundits I watched on TV handed investors a foolish advice, that is "to stay out of the market" unless they have 10 or more years to go before retirement. At that time, some of these investors have already lost 50% of their savings. Who knows how many took their advice and got out of the market thereby missing the strong bull market that started in March and is still going strong as of this minute. In January and February, many financial experts were predicting the Dow Jones Averages to go down to 5,000. In "DIDOSPIN-11,000 DOW, August 7, 2009" when DJIA was 9,370, I predicted the Dow to climb to 10,000 before the end of the year and to 11,000 before the end of next year. It already reached 10,000 last week. Most of the financial experts I watched on the Lou Dobbs and Larry Kudlow

Shows collectively stated that "it may take 10 years to recover losses in retirement plans…" Many of them created quips such as "your 401k has now turned into a 201k…" to scare investors. Shame on them for being so incompetent or for perpetrating a hoax! Those investors who stayed put have already gained back most of what they have lost and I believe this bull market still has legs before the next significant market correction.

In "DIDOSPIN- Obama's Recession, March 8, 2009", I said "Recessions are part of a normal economic cycle. Soon consumers will come back and resume buying necessities such as refrigerators, TVs, computers, furniture, cars…" How true! A lower than expected contraction in GDP at 1% in the 2nd quarter is believed to have been followed by a small positive increase in GDP in the 3rd quarter, although official stats have not yet been released. I predicted a much bigger increase in GDP the 4th quarter. The increase in GDP is an indication of an increase in consumer spending. **One thing to remember is that GDP stats do not even take into consideration business to business consumption, only the consumption of the ultimate consumer or end-user. This is something that many people are not aware of.**

I secretly scoffed at my boss in January when he told me in a panic that we must dig in our heels in this "worst ever recession". I told him, "We've seen this before, the last one in 2001…." "No, no, no", he adamantly replied, "this is different". How wrong he was! The only difference between this recession and the previous ones is its nickname. This one will probably be known by several nicknames such as "Sub-prime Mortgage Crisis, aka Housing Bubble Burst, aka Auto Industry Crisis Recession, aka as The Great Recession". The various nicknames given to the 3 previous recessions according to Bloomberg News were: Dot-Com Bubble Burst – 2000 to 2001; S&L Crisis, 1990 to 1991 and the Energy Crisis Recession, 1981 to 1982.

I concede that this will prove to be the longest recession since the Great Depression. But its severity and misery index pales in comparison to the Carter-Reagan recession. According to Bloomberg News, during the 1981-1982 recession, the national unemployment rate was 10.8% at its highest; inflation was 14% and the prime rate went up to 20.5%. In this current recession, inflation is almost non-existent and the prime rate is the lowest it has been in 50 years, source: http://www.wsjprimerate.us/wall_street_journal_prime_rate_history.htm

Obama's economists projected the unemployment rate will continue to increase and will exceed 10% before the year is over but I will go with my prediction in "DIDOSPIN- Recession Over, June 27, 2009" that it would peak at 9.8%. This means that more than 90% of the working population is employed and is poised to go back into the "buying mode". It is a cycle and consumers eventually buy what they need or want. The stock market rally is a big factor in consumer spending. If a consumer sees his portfolio going up in value, he will have more confidence spending his discretionary income as opposed to saving it for a rainy day. Fortunately, the behavior of the stock market follows a free market pattern that is predictable. The stock market does not like government intervention in the free market economy. It does not like redistribution of wealth; tax increases; government take-over of health care, the banking system and other private industries; cap and trade; interest hikes and increase in deficits. One of the reasons the market is doing so well is that Obamacare and Cap and Trade appear to be in trouble. There are different versions of Obamacare bills that are still under discussion in the congressional committees, and although Cap and Trade bill passed the house, it is not expected to pass the senate.

****end of article*****************************

"Being wealthy isn't just a question of having lots of money. It's a question of what we want. Every time we seek something that we can't afford, we can be counted as poor…"
―― Jean-Jacques Rousseau

Lie #1 – It's impossible to time the market……….

Whomever said this first and all the people that keep repeating it are either lying or just misinformed. Of course you can time the market and outperform the major stock market indices. Here is the magic formula:

1. Invest your money as shown in the book, ***"6m$Retiree"***, Chapter, ***"Asset Allocation"***,

2. Never go in and out of the stock market in times of recoveries (economic expansions). Do not touch your money. Leave your money alone even if there are market corrections of 10% to 30%.

3. Take your money out of the stock market ONLY before the start of the bear market that follows a recession. See the timeline showing approximately when you should bail out of equities in Chapter, ***"Inverted Yield Curve…"***

4. Follow the same timeline on the chart as to when you should get back into the stock market.

Pinpointing the official start of a recession……….

At the time of writing, the total of my 401k account is 100% invested in equities. I can honestly say that I have never lost money in the stock market. The reason is I know the behavior of the stock market---it goes up, it goes down. Historically, in a period of expansion there is a correction of 10% or more every 6 to 12 months. There is a correction of 20% or more every 12 to 18 months. I only check my account when the market is up. I am in for the long term and don't need my money now so why will I stress myself out checking my balance after the Dow goes down 500 points? I know my balance went down. Will it make me feel better to know by how much? Will I turn my paper loss into a real loss? Of course not! What I look out for are signs of a recession. The stock market can turn from boom to bust in just a few weeks during the bear market that follows a recession. Stocks may plunge 60% or more from their recent highs by the time the bear market bottom is reached. For the benefit of the reader who is not sure of the meaning of a recession, a recession is part of a normal business cycle. The economy expands and contracts (shrinks). A recession is a period of contraction. There will be periods of contraction caused by many different factors. But the simplest explanation is, the consumer stops consuming for a brief period of time, as in "recess" in school, i.e. a brief break between the usual activities. The most common financial definition of a recession is "two consecutive quarters of negative growth". The NBER (National Bureau of Economic Research) indicates in its website that this is not the official definition and that only its panel of experts can declare an "official recession" after taking into account a number of monthly factors such as employment, personal income, industrial production as well as quarterly GDP growth. This means that we could be a year into a recession before this panel of experts declares it official. This is exactly what happened during the "great recession" of 2007-2009. By historical accounts, the recession started in December 2007 and the NBER did not call the recession until December 1, 2008. That day the Dow closed at 8,149, 42.5% lower than its most recent peak of 14,164 in October 2007. Then it took the NBER's experts another year before they figured out that the recession ended in June 2009. I like using the DJIA as a barometer of market trend. It is an index of 30 large public companies in diversified industries making it a broader representation of how the U.S. economy and markets are currently trending. In general I use the DJIA, S&P 500 and NASDAQ as the major indices to gauge overall U.S. market performance.

Inverted yield curve, a harbinger of gloom and doom……….

During the great recession my holdings increased by more than 50% in just one year, 2009 by following a system that enabled me to get out of equities before stock prices collapsed and to get back into the same mutual funds close to the bottom of the bear market. **An inverted yield curve (aka Negative Yield Curve) is one of the best and most reliable early indicators of a recession. According to historical data, the yield curve inverted just prior to every U.S. recession in the past 50 years.** The Positive Yield (interest rate earned) Curve is the normal yield for investments. Longer term maturities usually have a higher yield than shorter term. When the yield becomes negative or inverted, market sentiment suggests that the long-term outlook is poor and the yields offered by long-term fixed income will continue to fall. It also spells trouble for the financial sector as what started happening in late 2006. The incentive for depositors to leave their money with the bank for longer periods of time, say 5 to 10 years is to earn a higher interest rate. If the interest rate of return is the same or less for 5 years compared to 1 year, this incentive is gone. This means that profit margins fall for companies that borrow cash at short-term rates and lend at long-term rates, such as hedge funds, banks and mortgage companies. Equity lines of credit and adjustable rate mortgages (ARMs) which are periodically adjusted usually go up since they are based on short-term interest rates. Debtors who got stuck with these loans will need more money to pay for additional interest. They will need to tighten their belts. They will have less money to spend on consumer goods that is why recessions follow an inverted yield curve.

The yield curve is inverted when short-term interest rates on U.S. Treasuries (T-bills) are higher than long term rates (T-notes and T-bonds). Check out the website below:

https://www.treasury.gov/resource-center/data-chart-center/interest-rates/Pages/TextView.aspx?data=yield

As of April 21, 2016, in accordance with the following table from the aforementioned website, the yield curve is not in any danger of flattening:

Date	1 mo	3 mo	6 mo	1 yr	2 yr	3 yr	5 yr	7 yr	10 yr	20 yr	30 yr
4/1/2016	0.2	0.23	0.4	0.6	0.8	0.9	1.2	1.6	1.79	2.2	2.62
4/4/2016	0.18	0.23	0.38	0.6	0.8	0.9	1.2	1.5	1.78	2.19	2.6
4/5/2016	0.19	0.23	0.36	0.6	0.7	0.9	1.2	1.5	1.73	2.13	2.54
4/6/2016	0.19	0.23	0.36	0.6	0.7	0.9	1.2	1.5	1.76	2.17	2.58
4/7/2016	0.2	0.23	0.36	0.5	0.7	0.8	1.1	1.5	1.7	2.1	2.52
4/8/2016	0.2	0.23	0.34	0.5	0.7	0.8	1.2	1.5	1.72	2.13	2.55
4/11/2016	0.19	0.23	0.34	0.5	0.7	0.9	1.2	1.5	1.73	2.14	2.56
4/12/2016	0.21	0.22	0.34	0.5	0.7	0.9	1.2	1.5	1.79	2.18	2.61
4/13/2016	0.21	0.23	0.36	0.6	0.8	0.9	1.2	1.5	1.77	2.16	2.58
4/14/2016	0.21	0.22	0.37	0.6	0.8	0.9	1.3	1.6	1.8	2.18	2.61
4/15/2016	0.19	0.22	0.37	0.5	0.7	0.9	1.2	1.5	1.76	2.14	2.56
4/18/2016	0.16	0.22	0.35	0.5	0.8	0.9	1.2	1.5	1.78	2.17	2.58
4/19/2016	0.18	0.21	0.36	0.5	0.8	0.9	1.3	1.6	1.79	2.19	2.6
4/20/2016	0.18	0.23	0.36	0.5	0.8	1	1.3	1.6	1.85	2.25	2.66
4/21/2016	0.19	0.23	0.37	0.6	0.8	1	1.4	1.7	1.88	2.29	2.69

Thursday Apr 21, 2016

The above chart shows 5-year rates are more than double that of the one-year rate, i.e. .6% vs. 1.4% and the 10-year rate is more than triple the one-year rate, i.e. .6% vs. 1.88%. This could mean we are still at least a year away from a negative yield curve. A recession would usually follow within 12 to 18 months of such an event, if history repeats itself. It is prudent to watch the chart diligently. Although the yield curve seems comfortably positive at the moment, the very low long term rates are a reason for concern. This is an indication that the markets think low inflation and low interest rates will continue. Low inflation and low interest rates can mean low growth and slow expansion. We may be experiencing a "new normal" like what Japan has been experiencing since the early nineties, i.e. sluggish growth of 1% to 3% GDP per year with the economy ever teetering on the brink of recession. Low interest rates is always good for stocks because even the most conservative investors have no appetite for treasuries, bonds, money market funds and bank CDs that pay zero to 3% annual yield. Consequently, they have to take a chance on equities.

The yield curve inverted on July 17, 2006 (Inversion) when the 10-year note (T-note) yielded 5.06% and the 3-month bill (T-bill) yielded 5.11%. From a historical perspective, I knew a recession would follow within the next 12 to 18 months so I got out of equities in August 2007 when the Dow was about 13,200 and I put my entire portfolio into a money market fund. At the risk of being redundant, this statement is repeated several times in this book. Repetition and reinforcement of this message may lead to clarity, especially for readers who are not familiar with the yield curve. That was a defensive capital preservation move. I must admit that I was tempted to go back in when the Dow closed at around 14,100 sometime in October 2007. I thought I got out too soon, but it is a good thing I did not. From that high, the Dow steadily declined until it plunged thousands of points between September and November 2008. I bought back in after the NBER announced the official date of the recession, which according to them started sometime in December 2007. I got back into equities the day after the NBER made the announcement. I was fully invested in the stock market, 100% in equities on December 2, 2008 when the Dow closed at 8,419. With this move, I avoided a 4,781 point value loss in the Dow. Of course I could have taken a chance by waiting a month or two before going back into the market after the declaration. An assumption can be made that the declaration of the official date of the recession by the NBER will initially cause more panic selling. If I waited till February 2009 I would have gotten back in closer to the bottom of the bear market, but I'm happy with my end result. I got out of the market not far from the peak and got back in not far from bottom.

Historically this is what happens: A bear market always lags behind a recession. A bull market always runs ahead of a recovery (end of the recession). How do you know when to get back into the market? A bull market starts a few months before a recession ends. It is difficult for financial advisors and economists to predict that a recession is near its end. They rely on economic data that is outdated when it becomes available. Economists have a terrible track record of forecasting the start and the end of recessions. This is evidenced by the foolish advice of many commentators, financial professionals, economists and other experts, for investors to stay out of equities in 2009. All you have to do is rewind the programs Larry Kudlow Show, Mad Money, Lou Dobbs Show, Squawk Box, Nightline and Bloomberg News. During the first quarter of 2009, I watched daily commentaries from financial expert after financial expert. Their collective advice was for investors to stay out of the stock market "if they cannot afford to lose any of their money". The problem with that advice is that most stock market investors have already lost 50% of their money by that time. And frankly, who can really afford to lose any of their money? These financial experts were caught napping in 2009 and missed the strongest bull market in history when stocks suddenly reversed course and kept going up recovering 60% of their value from the bear market bottom of March 2009. It is important to study the charts carefully so that you can get back into stocks before the start of the bull market that precedes the end of the recession. The timeline on the first chart illustrates DJIA closing prices from July 17, 2006 (Inversion) when the negative yield curve started until the recession ended in June 2009:

DJIA INDEX - HISTORY		
Date	Closing Price	
7/17/2006	10,747	Start of negative yield curve
7/17/2007	13,972	1 year anniversary of negative yield curve
7/18/2007	13,918	
7/19/2007	14,000	
7/20/2007	13,851	
7/23/2007	13,943	
7/24/2007	13,717	
7/25/2007	13,785	
7/26/2007	13,474	
7/27/2007	13,265	
7/30/2007	13,358	
7/31/2007	13,212	
8/1/2007	13,362	
8/2/2007	13,463	
8/3/2007	13,182	
8/6/2007	13,469	
8/7/2007	13,504	
8/8/2007	13,658	
8/9/2007	13,271	
8/10/2007	13,240	
8/13/2007	13,237	
8/14/2007	13,029	
8/15/2007	12,861	

Date	Value
8/16/2007	12,846
8/17/2007	13,079
8/20/2007	13,121
8/21/2007	13,091
8/22/2007	13,236
8/23/2007	13,236
8/24/2007	13,379
8/27/2007	13,322
8/28/2007	13,042
8/29/2007	13,289
8/30/2007	13,239
8/31/2007	13,358
9/4/2007	13,449
9/5/2007	13,305
9/6/2007	13,363
9/7/2007	13,113
9/10/2007	13,128
9/11/2007	13,308
9/12/2007	13,292
9/13/2007	13,425
9/14/2007	13,443
9/17/2007	13,403
9/18/2007	13,739
9/19/2007	13,816
9/20/2007	13,767
9/21/2007	13,820
9/24/2007	13,759

Date	Value		
9/25/2007	13,779		
9/26/2007	13,878		
9/27/2007	13,913		
9/28/2007	13,896		
10/1/2007	14,088		
10/2/2007	14,047		
10/3/2007	13,968		
10/4/2007	13,974		
10/5/2007	14,066		
10/8/2007	14,044		
10/9/2007	14,165		
10/10/2007	14,079		
10/11/2007	14,015		
10/12/2007	14,093		
10/15/2007	13,985		
10/16/2007	13,913		Historically, recession may start on any of these dates
10/17/2007	13,893		
10/18/2007	13,889		
10/19/2007	13,522		
10/22/2007	13,567		
10/23/2007	13,676		
10/24/2007	13,675		
10/25/2007	13,672		
10/26/2007	13,807		
10/29/2007	13,870		
10/30/2007	13,792		
10/31/2007	13,930		

Date	Value	
11/1/2007	13,568	
11/2/2007	13,595	
11/5/2007	13,543	
11/6/2007	13,661	
11/7/2007	13,300	
11/8/2007	13,266	
11/9/2007	13,043	
11/12/2007	12,988	
11/13/2007	13,307	
11/14/2007	13,231	
11/15/2007	13,110	
11/16/2007	13,177	
11/19/2007	12,958	
11/20/2007	13,010	
11/21/2007	12,799	
11/23/2007	12,981	
11/26/2007	12,743	
11/27/2007	12,958	
11/28/2007	13,289	
11/29/2007	13,312	
11/30/2007	13,372	
12/3/2007	13,315	Start of recession according to NBER - Dec 2007
12/4/2007	13,249	
12/5/2007	13,445	
12/6/2007	13,620	
12/7/2007	13,626	

Date	Value
12/10/2007	13,727
12/11/2007	13,433
12/12/2007	13,474
12/13/2007	13,518
12/14/2007	13,340
12/17/2007	13,167
12/18/2007	13,232
12/19/2007	13,207
12/20/2007	13,246
12/21/2007	13,451
12/24/2007	13,550
12/26/2007	13,552
12/27/2007	13,360
12/28/2007	13,366
12/31/2007	13,265
1/2/2008	13,044
1/3/2008	13,057
1/4/2008	12,800
1/7/2008	12,827
1/8/2008	12,589
1/9/2008	12,735
1/10/2008	12,853
1/11/2008	12,606
1/14/2008	12,778
1/15/2008	12,501
1/16/2008	12,466
1/17/2008	12,159

RECESSION OF 2007-2009 SIGNIFICANT DATES			
	DOW Closing Price		
7/17/2006	10,747	Start of negative yield curve	
7/17/2007	13,972	Anniversary of negative yield curve	SELL
8/9/2007	13,271	End of negative yield curve (almost 13 mos. since inversion)	
10/9/2007	14,165	Peak since inversion	
12/3/2007	13,315	Official start of recession (declared in Dec 2008)	
9/17/2008	10,610	Start of the bear market	
12/1/2008	8,149	On this date NBER declares recession started in Dec 2007	BUY
3/9/2009	6,547	Bear market bottom	
4/9/2009	8,083	Start of bull market	
6/1/2009	8,721	Official end of recession per NBER	
12/31/2009	10,428	Year end, bull market continues	

According to the chart, the markets continued to go up after the yield curve inverted until the Dow peaked at 14,165 on October 9, 2007, about 14 months from inversion date. Then the bear market started on September 17, 2008, 9 months after the recession began. The bear market reached bottom at 6,547 on March 9, 2009. If you had a crystal ball, sold at the peak and bought at the bottom, your assets would have increased by an astounding 75% by the end of 2009. I did not make quite as much but I'm satisfied. See the details under the chapter, **"How I earned more than 50% return on my money in just one year"**. If you follow my system you would have sold on July 17, 2007 when the DOW closed at 13,972 and bought back into the same mutual funds on December 1, 2008 when the DOW closed at 8,149 thereby avoiding a 5,823 point loss on the DOW.

Here is the summary of the Arthur V. Prosper timing system:

- Allocate your investments as shown in the book, ***6m$Retiree***, Chapter, "Asset Allocation",
- Do not touch your investments in times of economic expansions (recoveries). Leave your money alone even if your portfolio loses 30% of its value.
- Monitor the Daily Treasury Yield Curve Rates at least once a month. Click on the website below: https://www.treasury.gov/resource-center/data-chart-center/interest-rates/Pages/TextView.aspx?data=yieldYear&year=2016 Specifically, compare the 10-year note yield to that of the 3-month bill. Watch carefully if the yields are starting to narrow and flatten.
- When the yield curve inverts, i.e. the 10-year treasury yield falls below the 3-month yield, make note of that date and continue to monitor to see if the inverted yield curve continues. Keep your ears open for news on what action

the Feds (Federal Reserve Bank) will take. Most likely, if the Feds increase the benchmark interest rate, the inverted yield curve will continue. If they decrease the benchmark rate, the inverted yield curve will end.
- If the yield curve stays inverted for over a month, make a note of the inversion date. Get out of the stock market when the inverted yield curve ends or when it reaches its one year anniversary whichever is earlier. Sell your stocks and put them in a money market fund or a stable value fund where the principal is guaranteed. This is a defensive move for preservation of your capital so as to avoid the bear market that will follow.
- When the NBER declares that we are in a recession and points to the date when it started, and that date is at least 6 months prior to the announcement date, put your money back into the same mutual funds they were in before you left the market.

Let us examine how your investments would have done in the Recession of 2001 if you followed my system. Review the following chart:

RECESSION OF 2001 SIGNIFICANT DATES

Date	Dow Closing Price		
7/7/2000	10,636	Start of neg yield curve	
9/6/2000	11,311	Most recent high since inversion	
2/12/2001	10,947	End of neg yield curve	SELL
3/1/2001	10,450	Start of recession	
7/6/2001	10,253	1 year anniversary negative curve	
11/28/2001	9,712	On this date NBER declares recession started Mar 2001	BUY
11/30/2001	9,852	End of recession	
10/9/2002	7,286	Bottom of bear market	
3/17/2003	8,142	Start of the bull market	

If you followed my system, you would have sold on or about February 12, 2001 when the DOW closed at 10,947 and bought back into the same mutual funds on or about November 28, 2001 when the DOW closed at 9,712. You would have avoided a 1,235 point decline in the DOW. It is important to remember that 2002 was a particularly difficult year for stock market investors. True to the rule that the bull market starts before the end of a recession, the bull market of 2001 actually started the beginning of October 2001 approximately 2 months before the end of the recession. But there was a major correction that started in the second quarter of 2002 that caused approximately a 30% stock market devaluation. Many economists surmised that the economy was going through a "W" shaped, double dipped recession but the economic indicators did not prove that to be the case. The country's steady recovery from the 9/11 attacks and the proclamation of many economists in November 2001 that the recession was about to end, created a healthy bump in share prices that continued until towards the middle of the second quarter of 2002. In June 2002 stock prices took a sharp downturn with the DOW plunging thousands of points to a low of 7,286 in October, losing 30% of its value from the beginning of the year. Tech stocks were especially devastated with the NASDAQ plunging from its 2000 high of 5,048 to a low of 1,114 in 2002. Most economists view this exceptionally tough year for the stock market as part of a correction after the decade long bull market that led to unusually high stock valuations. But still, you would have been better off than most investors if you followed my system.

False negative..........

If the yield curve inversion occurs then flip-flops from negative to positive during the 12-month period that follows the first inversion from positive to negative, watch the yield curve carefully. If we take the last inversion as an example, the yield curve first inverted on December 22, 2005. Let us call this date a FND (False Negative Date). The rate on a 2 year Treasury bill became higher than a 7 year Treasury note. When this occurs, the corrective action from the Federal Reserve is to lower rates but the opposite happened. The Feds continued to raise interest rates. The yield curve fluctuated back and forth from negative to flat to negative until July 17, 2006 when the yield curve inverted and stayed inverted until towards the end of 2008. By that time the NBER declared that we were a year into a recession and the major market indices showed we were in the middle of a brutal bear market. If you got out of the stock market a year after the FND, on December 22, 2006, the Dow closing price was 12,343. If you followed my strategy you would have bought back into the market on December 2, 2008 when the Dow closed at 8,419. You would have avoided a 3,924 point devaluation of the Dow and gained 3,900 points increase by the end of 2009. Still not too shabby even if you got out of the market on the FND. The danger is that the yield curve may get back to normal (positive) and stave off a recession. So in this respect, it is better to watch for a "true negative", then develop a timeline. A true negative, as defined in this strategy, is when the yield curve inverts and stays inverted for a year. Especially when the 10-year Treasury yield falls below the yield on 3-month treasury bills. When this happens the economy will either be in a recession or close to it. An analytical reader will probably ask, "So, if I get out of the stock market and stayed out for two years, won't I lose 2 years' earnings?" The answer is maybe yes, maybe no. There will be so much volatility in the market the year before a recession hits. There will be wild swings and fluctuations between losses and gains in the major indices. It is likely that you will get out of stocks at the wrong time if you do not follow the timeline. It will be less stressful for you if you sell out earlier rather than later. Take comfort in the knowledge that you will be immune from "the crash" when it happens. Rather than worry, spend your time doing other pleasurable things in life. Play golf, the piano, go to the movies and parties, play with your children, take vacations or find a hobby. Just keep your ears open for the proclamation from the NBER of the official date of the recession. Get back into equities within a month of the official declaration and buy back the stocks you sold at their depreciated price.

How to lose 60% in the stock market……….

My financial advisor (licensed stock broker) whom we shall call by the name of Rebecca was one of those stock market investors who lost a lot of money during the great recession. In July 2008 Rebecca had her money, close to a million dollars of it, equally divided between a diversified emerging markets fund, a mid-cap growth fund, a large value fund, a specialty natural resources fund and a specialty real estate fund. If you are a stock broker you know which funds I am talking about. Rebecca was very aggressive in her investment choices, bordering almost on reckless and speculative. Well, she paid the price.

We parted ways around the time the interest yield curve started flattening. We had many discussions about the state of the economy and disagreed on how my money should be invested. I told her that I am concerned the interest rate curve inverted from positive to negative and historically…to make a long story short, I fired her. Our paths crossed again around the middle of 2009 at a cocktail party that was hosted by one of the largest banks in the nation that shall remain nameless but whose initials are HSBC. After 3 or 4 Margaritas, she told me her story. She thought her investments along with her clients' investments were doing "OK", with losses of less than 20% for the year at that point. Then President Bush delivered his speech on September 24, 2008 announcing the government's bailout of banks with toxic assets. She thought the president's speech caused more of a panic in the market which precipitated an abrupt panic selling. To make her situation worse, she sold all her stocks on or about October 10, 2008 after the Dow plunged approximately 2,500 points between September 25 and October 9, 2008. She thought stocks would continue to go down. But when the Dow gained about 900 points on October 28, 2008, she put her money back into the same 5 funds they were in before. She thought the bear market was close to bottom and stocks would start going up. But stocks kept going down. On or about November 20, 2008, she took what was left of her money out of the market again and put it all in a money market fund, now convinced that the bottom of the bear market has a long way to go. When we met at that cocktail party in mid-2009, all her money was still in a money market fund. None of her money was invested in equities. She did not know that the recession ended (no one knew) and that we were in the middle of the biggest bull market in history. Indeed the NBER did not proclaim, until a year later, that the recession ended in June 2009. That was how she lost 60% of the value of her portfolio. You would think a stock broker knows enough about the stock market to NOT lose 60%. It's a dirty little secret. But the truth is that many stock brokers, financial advisors, investment brokers, economists, speculators, finance gurus, hedge fund managers, market watchers, business forecasters, best-selling authors and the so-called stock market geniuses lost money in the last recession just like most people. Warren Buffett lost $25 billion in the 2007-2009 recession cutting his fortune from $62 billion to $37 billion. It is my opinion and belief that the holdings of best-selling Amazon Kindle Books finance advice authors Dave Ramsey, Suze Orman and JC Bogle all lost money from the start of the bear market until it ended…that is if I go by their credo of "Buy right, hold tight and stay the course". Billionaire Carl Icahn, Andrew Smithers, Paul B. Farrell and James Dale Davidson must have lost a lot of money this year if they followed their own advice to get out of stocks before "the crash" that they predicted WILL happen in 2016.

    My last contact with Rebecca was towards the end of 2013 when she told me over the phone that she has not yet recovered all the money she lost during the last recession…"good I'm not yet forty five, so I still have plenty of time to recover the money before I retire.." she cheerfully said. I'm glad above it all, she had a cavalier attitude about losing 60% of her money. I LOL, though I never made any disparaging remark. I could have told her, "…and I was paying you 2% for financial advice when I made over 50% return on my money by the time the great recession ended?!!"

I was surprised when I found out that many of Bernie Madoff's clients were banks, financial institutions and asset management firms. He duped banks, firms and other financial institutions domiciled in Spain, Scotland, Austria, Japan, Switzerland, the Netherlands, France, Italy, Portugal and Singapore (source: http://www.townandcountrymag.com/society/money-and-power/a9656715/bernie-madoff-ponzi-scheme-scandal-story-and-aftermath/).

The founder of Bed, Bath and Beyond, the owner of the NY Mets, the IOC and many schools and universities gave him their money to invest. All he did was give his clients quarterly statements showing that their investments made 12% to 20% returns no matter how the markets moved. Had it not been for the financial crisis of 2008 in which many of his clients wanted to withdraw their money, Madoff's Ponzi scheme could have gone on indefinitely. Madoff's case is indeed a study in greed but most of all it's a study in human gullibility, that even the most astute financial professionals can be duped out of millions of dollars. So there, I will manage my own finances, thank you.

"It was not curiosity that killed the goose who laid the golden egg, but an insatiable greed that devoured common sense."

— E.A. Bucchianeri, Brushstrokes of a Gadfly

How I earned more than 50% return on my money in just one year……….

     I face the same challenges as everyone else. But I am a simple man with simple aspirations and ambitions in life. I will be perfectly happy to spend my retirement years fishing, then cooking my catch and finding ways to help my community. My most precious possession is my health. That is why I prefer a stress-free investment strategy. Stress and anxiety can mess up your mind, distort your judgment and cause emotional distress which can lead to depression and a weakened immune system. Suicides increased to 18.9 per 100,000 in 1929 in the year of Wall Street's crash. Some studies correlate economic hardship and increased suicides (source: http://www.huffingtonpost.com/2014/06/13/suicide-recession_n_5491687.html). Fundamentally, there is nothing wrong with the investment strategy of many financial experts to "buy, hold and stay the course", come hell or high water. But I believe that the component I've added to this strategy of getting out of stocks to escape the bear market that follows a recession will not add much stress and anxiety to your life.

     I fared well during the last recession based on the very basic knowledge I have about the economy and the stock market combined with my knowledge of history. All you have to watch for is the flattening then inverting of the yield curve. My 401k retirement savings was fully invested in the stock market equally allocated into these five mutual funds: Black Rock Natural Resources, Oppenheimer Developing Markets, AF Euro Pacific Growth, Columbia Acorn Mid-cap and AF Growth Fund. I sold my stocks following my timing strategy and bought them back on December 2, 2008. By the end of 2009, the balance of my portfolio increased by more than 50%. This is after backing out new contributions and their earnings. Exiting the stock market then going back into the same funds you were in before, simply means your money will buy more shares of the same depreciated stock. The following two charts are examples of how the increase in value of your holdings is calculated:

Mutual Fund 1			PPS		Shares	Total
Jul	17	2006	$ 52	INVERSION		
Jul	17	2007	$ 61	ANNIVERSARY OF INVERSION		
Aug	13	2007	$ 58	GOT OUT OF STOCKS	5,000	290,000.00
Dec	01	2008	$ 30	NBER DECLARED RECESSION STARTED DEC 2007		
Dec	02	2008	$ 31	GOT BACK INTO STOCKS	9,355	290,000.00
Dec	30	2009	$ 50	BALANCE IN THIS FUND AS OF THIS DATE	9,355	467,750.00
				$ INCREASE IN VALUE		$ 177,750.00
				% INCREASE IN VALUE		61.3%

Mutual Fund 2	PPS		Shares	Total
Jul 17, 2006	$ 36	INVERSION		
Jul 17, 2007	$ 44	ANNIVERSARY OF INVERSION		
Aug 13, 2007	$ 40	GOT OUT OF STOCKS	5,000	200,000.00
Dec 01, 2008	$ 20	NBER DECLARED RECESSION STARTED DEC 2007		
Dec 02, 2008	$ 21	GOT BACK INTO STOCKS	9,524	200,004.00
Dec 30, 2009	$ 30	BALANCE IN THIS FUND AS OF THIS DATE	9,524	285,720.00
		$ INCREASE IN VALUE		$ 85,720.00
		% INCREASE IN VALUE		42.9%

The aforementioned tables are only representations of my financial position during the time indicated. They are not my real portfolio.

Recessions are a normal part of a never ending economic cycle. They are inevitable in a free market economy and they are short lived. There will be brief periods when consumers will stop purchasing non-essential goods, then resume their usual buying pattern. Post World War II U.S. recessions have lasted an average of 10 months. The worst thing you can do is to sell your stocks after they have lost 50%. Many certified financial planners (CFPs) are tricky. It was unfortunate that my brother got stuck with one during the great recession of 2007-2009. After my brother's portfolio was cut in half, the advisor directed my brother to get his money out of the stock market and put his entire (depreciated) holdings, 50% into a money market fund and 50% into treasuries. Towards the end of 2009, my brother complained to the financial advisor that he lost a lot of money. The advisor replied, "You really did not lose a penny. You just did not make much..." My brother almost smacked him in the face. Why tell your clients to get out of the stock market after stocks declined more than 50%? In all seriousness, missing a rally of that magnitude in 2009 was a serious error in judgment on the part of the financial planner. My holdings grew by more than 50% in 2009 while my brother's earned a measly 4% APR. I've done a lot better on my own than when my portfolio was in the hands of my financial advisors. I worked with two CFPs successively and the best result they produced for me was a 9.5% annual yield and that was on a good year when the bulls were running and everyone else was making 17%. I have been doing much better on my own since I fired them. The new fiduciary rules released on April 6, 2016 by the U.S. Department of Labor which does not go into full effect until 2018 requires a financial advisor to place the client's interest first when making recommendations for investing their retirement savings, 401k and/or IRA accounts. The fiduciary's recommendations must not be influenced by the amount or type of compensation he or she receives. I doubt that this would help much. All the fiduciary has to do is make the client sign a disclosure form called "best interest contract exemption" (BICE) which describes how the advisor is paid, e.g. by commission or as a percent of the total investment, and state why the product he sold is in the best interest of the client. An investor usually signs anything that is put in front of him. It would be no different than signing the "suitable investment disclosure" that fiduciaries currently ask clients to sign.

Let us review the lesson..........

1) An inverted yield curve is a reliable sign of an oncoming recession. 2) The stock market will lose 30% to 60% of its value when a recession hits. 3) Post WWII recessions are short-lived. They last an average of 10 months. 4) When the NBER formally declares a recession, it may already be ending or it has already ended. It happened this way in the recessions of 2007-2009, 2001 and 1990-1991. 5) A bull market is always ahead of the recovery. A bear market always lags an oncoming recession. To simplify this, a bear market starts when a recession is already in full bloom and the bull market will begin months before the end of that particular recession.

If you can get out of stocks a year before the start of a bear market that follows a recession, like I did, and get back into stocks after the NBER makes an official announcement designating the approximate date of the recession, like I did, you will be very happy. You will avoid the crash. This is sort of like "getting to heaven before the devil finds out you're dead". To help you beat the devil, here are other signs of a recession that you can look out for in no particular order: Reduction in the price of Copper to below $2 per pound; a sustained increase in initial jobless claims and declining job growth; a continuous decline in factory orders, housing starts, existing home sales, industrial production, retail sales and consumer confidence index. A steady decline in consumer spending followed by a sharp drop in commodity prices. If any of these economic indicators persist week after week, a recession is on the horizon. An increase in the Federal Reserve benchmark interest rate in the face of declining indices may be enough to push the economy into a recession. Fed Reserve Chairperson Janet Yellen has been very cautious in raising interest rates. Her conservative monetary policy has been working so as to avoid another recession. She seems to be an independent thinker who is committed in maintaining a goldilocks economy which the market likes. She made it clear in a speech at the Jackson Hole economic symposium in 2014 that she would not arbitrarily follow The Taylor Rule (http://www.businessinsider.com/yellen-on-taylor-rule-jackson-hole-2014-8) which many economists contend stabilizes monetary policy. Indeed if she followed the Taylor rule, she could have raised the Fed rates by an additional 50 basis points every year in 2014, 2015 and in 2016 based on the low inflation and low unemployment rates and the overall economy, in theory, would have been much stronger but there is also a danger that the recovery would be truncated. As it is, with the Fed policy of "lower rates longer", a decade long (or longer) bull market is foreseeable.

Let us suppose you can get out of the stock market before the bear market starts, how do you know when to get back into stocks again? How can you hit the bullseye the second time? Here are signs that the bear market is ending or has ended: The NBER officially declared a recession and pointed to its start; It has been at least 6 months since that date; The Dow has gone down more than 30% from its most recent high; Most of the economic indicators are pointing upwards; Major stock market indices stopped fluctuating wildly and post weekly gains several weeks in a row, pointing to an impending bull market.

"Every day is a bank account, and time is our currency. No one is rich, no one is poor, we've got 24 hours each."
― Christopher Rice

PART III – LET "TIME" WORK FOR YOU……….

The KISS Principle and Auto-Pilot Strategy……….

We have seen the magic of compounding in previous chapters. If investors invested their money and just left it alone and let time work its magic, that money would grow to amazing proportions. At a tender age of 30, one might think 37 years is a lifetime to wait for money to grow into $3.3 million. But life on earth is brief. Time will fly with little notice.

Investing should be simple. The "KISS Principle" works well as an investment strategy. For the reader who has never heard of this acronym, it can mean a few things: Keep it short and simple, keep it small and simple, keep it simple and straightforward but my favorite variation of it is "keep it simple stupid". The average investor like you and me should not be inundated with jargon such as: leverage, derivatives, future risk, exchange, multiple streams, codility, doji, secular bear market, quadratic vector, marginal cost, hedgehog forecasting, dark pool, contra market, hot asset class, accidental high yielder, standard deviation, shorting, market kinematics, AQR Risk Parity, Sharpe ratio, etc. etc. etc. If you hired a financial professional and he keeps using such jargon, run the other way. Investing should not cause unnecessary stress and anxiety. It should not keep you awake at night. You will make more money using the KISS principle than getting in and out of stocks during dips and rises in stocks in a period of economic boom. Most investors will never manage to get out of stocks before a major correction. If you failed to follow my timing system to get out of the market before the bust, you will be better off to just leave your money alone until the next boom. If the average investors who lost 50% of their holdings in March 2009 kept it simple and left their money where it was, they would have recovered all of their losses within 2 ½ years. Those who listened to bad investment advice and took their money out of equities and got back in only at the end of 2009, did not recover the pre-recession value of their portfolio until after 6 years. For the average investor, it is never a good idea to try to time the market unless you are following the strategy in this book. Buying low and selling high and trading all day long is for stock brokers who do it for a living and are prepared to take that certain amount of stress built into their occupations. For the average investor, if you cannot follow my strategy to get out of stocks before the beginning of the bear market that follows a recession and get back in at the start of the bull market when the recession is about to end, you will be better off with the "auto-pilot strategy"---leave your money alone. Don't touch your money until you have to. You will do just as well as most other investors, making an average of 12% APY in the long run. If you learned from this book and hit the bullseye the first time, i.e. you got out of the market before the bear market started and you put all your money into a money market or stable fund, do not look at the stock market indices again (DJIA, S&P 500, NASDAQ, NYSE, VIX, etc. etc.) while you are out of the stock market. Block all the news from all your senses about how the major indices are doing. If you keep monitoring the market and keep seeing the major indices going up, it can be gut wrenching and the consequences can be disastrous. You might be tempted to go back in and might get caught with all your money back into equities while stocks are taking an even more severe downward spiral. Relax, sit back, watch TV and have a glass of beer or wine. Prepare yourself to be out of the stock market for 2 years. Take comfort in the knowledge that you will not lose 30% or more of your money when the next BIG ONE comes which it inevitably will. When the NBER declares the official start date of the recession and the major indices have plunged 30% to 60% from their most recent high, put your money back into the same mutual funds they were in before you got out of the stock market. You will not be far from the bottom of that bear market if you follow this strategy. See, Chapter, **"Investment Strategy and Asset Allocation"**.

Managing My Investment Portfolio – 30 minutes……….

I do not spend much time analyzing and worrying about current events that affect the market. Investing is not rocket science. I know that business, financial, political and economic news are market movers and will cause volatility in the market. So what's the point of worrying? I check the market indices thrice daily, at the opening bell at 9:30 AM, at 12:30 PM then again when the market closes at the end of the day. There is always volatility in the market. If Janet Yellen, Mario Draghi, Angela Merkel or Barack Obama delivers a speech about the economy, the market may go up or down. If there is a new round of quantitative easing (QE), the market will go up. If oil prices go down, the market may go up…or down. So what is the point of watching the market go up and down and stressing over paper losses of 10% to 20%? I am not going to take my money out if my portfolio goes down 20%. I am not going to take my money out if my portfolio goes up 20%. The stock market goes in cycles. Even in "good times" there will be profit taking by the Gnomes of Wall Street which may cause stocks to go down in value. When you sell your depreciated stocks, that is when the Gnomes will snatch them. Even professional stock market traders, wealth managers and hedge fund owners can lose a lot of money trying to time the market. Stock market experts themselves have difficulty trying to put together a winning portfolio of stocks, let alone time the market. "A blindfolded monkey throwing darts at a newspaper's financial pages could select a portfolio that would do just as well as one carefully selected by experts", wrote Burton Malkiel in his best seller, "A Random Walk down Wall Street". If you choose the wrong stocks like I did (see the next chapter), you can get wiped out. If you get out of equities at the wrong time, you can miss the best 10 days of a bull market. I probably do a lot better than many of the so-called experts with my auto-pilot strategy, to "buy-and-hold" during the boom cycle of the economy and to stay out of the stock market during the "bust cycle" when stocks returned a negative yield.

"If wealth was the inevitable result of hard work and enterprise, every woman in Africa would be a millionaire."
— George Monbiot

Isn't There a Better Investment Strategy?..........

I've tried many different investment strategies but I've had no luck. Because of my greed and daring nature, I managed to recklessly gamble away a big chunk of my fortune pursuing riskier investments such as buying rental properties and investing in individual stocks.

By way of example, sometime in October 2002, I got a "hot tip" from my brother in law about a company whose stocks were supposed to go through the roof. The company was Cisco Systems (CSCO). I had $20,000 cash in the bank earning very little interest so I decided to gamble on this tip and bought approximately 2,300 CSCO stocks at $8.50 each. I watched the stock price daily as it crept up. I heard a tip 2 months later that the stock will suddenly plunge so I got scared and sold my 2,300 stocks on December 2, 2002 when the stock price reached $15.06. I was congratulating myself for netting a cool profit of $15,000 in just 2 months but when I received the proceeds of the sale, the whole $35,000 of it, I asked myself, "what now?" Do I put the $35,000 back into a money market fund in my bank, buy stocks from another company or buy back the same stock? After much deliberation with myself, I decided that buying individual company stocks is not really a good investment strategy for anyone whose day job is not in stock trading because the "what now?" question will always be a dilemma. If you decide to dabble in trading individual company stocks, for every Monster Trade you make you will have 2, 3 or 4 losing trades. It's a hit or miss gambling proposition in the Wall Street Casino. For every Priceline, Apple and Amazon, there is a Tyco, WorldCom and Enron. I have decided that I want to live the rest of my life as stress-free as possible. So I have agreed with myself that that the simplest path to wealth is to leave my money alone during boom times, let time and yield work for me, then time the market to get out before the bust. My goal is to hit the bullseye twice:

First, to get out of the market before the start of the bear market that follows a recession. Second, to get back into the market before the start of the bull market. If you are able to stay close to the timeline of our timing strategy, it is possible to make 50% APY on your money during the first year of the recovery. For now until the yield curve inverts, there is nothing wrong with making an average return of 12% APY. See the following table showing an example of how your portfolio may end up using the Arthur V. Prosper system vs. the buy, hold and stay the course strategy:

Buy, hold and stay the course strategy:	
Sample value of portfolio before the start of the bear market that follows a recession	100,000
50% Loss of value during the bust	-50,000
Portfolio's value at the end of the bear market	50,000
50% Gain, 1ST year of recovery	25,000
Portfolio balance after first year of recovery	**$75,000**

Arthur V. Prosper Timing Strategy:	
Sample value of portfolio before the start of the bear market that follows a recession	100,000
0% Loss of value during the bust	0
Portfolio's value at the end of the bear market	100,000
50% Gain, 1ST year of recovery	50,000
Portfolio balance after first year of recovery	**$150,000**

Arthur V. Prosper's Timing Strategy beats the buy, hold and stay the course strategy by 100%

The following are some of the investment strategies I have tried which were beaten by the Arthur V. Prosper KISS Principle and Auto-Pilot Strategy:

- **Individual Stock Picking** – I came into some cash in the year 2000 from the sale of several rental properties. So I bought Yahoo at $90 in 2000 and had to sell it for $8 in 2002. I bought AOL for $109 in 2001 and had to sell it for $26 in 2002. I bought Intel at $65 in 2000 and had to sell it for $18 in 2002. I bought Ford at $26 in 2000 and had to sell it for $10 in 2002. Need I say more? Clearly individual stock picking is not for the ordinary investor like me. I squandered more than $200,000 of cash like it was monopoly money. Now I look at it as the tuition fee for the hard lesson I learned. If I had to do it over again, all I would do is use the cash to maximize my contribution to my 401k which is invested as shown under the chapter, **"Investment Strategy - Asset Allocation"**.

 For those of you who are about to retire, saved a substantial amount of money, say $2 million or more of cash and are hoping to live off the dividends and leave the principal to your heirs, and are not inclined to follow the Arthur V. Prosper System, check out high quality dividend paying stocks from solid companies with a record of profitability which are not likely to go out of business in this lifetime. Click on the website below for more information:
 http://www.dividend.com/
 For example, you can divide your $2 million equally into several quality dividend stocks that pay 3% to 5% such as Astra-Zeneca, Glaxo-Smith-Kline, Hanes Brands, Nike, Walt Disney, Apple, Microsoft, Intel Corp, Pepsi-Cola,

Coca-Cola, Johnson & Johnson, 3M Company, Proctor & Gamble, McDonald's, Hewlett-Packard, AT&T, Johnson Controls Inc., Exxon-Mobile, Chevron, Phillips, Stanley Black & Decker, Deere and IBM. You can live off the dividends and leave the principal alone to grow.

Please keep in mind that the above-mentioned companies are used as examples only and are not specifically recommended. Do your due diligence as to the financial strength and viability of each company.

- **Options Trading, Day Trading, Short Selling** – I took some courses at an online trading academy, a school that shall remain nameless. It was a total waste of time and money. For most people options trading, day trading and shorting is something that is better left as a complete mystery so as to avoid the unbelievable stress and real losses associated with this activity. Believe me this is not for the faint of heart. If you are one of those people who are avoiding stressful situations in their lives, this is not for you. Their advertising catch phrase, "You make money when the market is up and you can make money when the market is down" neglects the second phrase which should be: "You can lose a lot of money when the market is up or down". Of course it is common sense but I love the way they leave it up to you to figure it out. Bottom line is, you will never make more money in day trading and shorting than you would following The Arthur V. Prosper system.

- **Stop Loss Strategy** – I took this course after listening to Bill Bresnan's advice on his daily radio talk show. The strategy is to set up a stop-loss for your stocks or mutual funds to trigger a sell order when they have lost a pre-set percentage. It is sort of a red line to trigger a sell order. The stop-loss may be automatically timed but manual

monitoring is preferable. Your stocks may drop below the line during the day which will trigger the sell order but then regain their value by the time the market closes. It could become a real mess of frequent selling and buying…requiring a considerable amount of activity in a period of great volatility in the market. Nowadays, it is doubtful that this can even be done with the money inside your retirement account. Most mutual funds have severely limited the number of trades in a month. Some stop-loss setting percentages are 10%, 12%, 15%, 20%, etc. The stop-loss percentages depend on the volume and volatility of the stocks or mutual funds. This is a simple example of how it works: My stop-loss is 10%. The price of the stock is $1 at its most recent high. I sell the stock when it drops to $0.90. The idea behind a stop-loss strategy is that you are convinced that the stock price will continue to drop below the 10% decline you have set, thereby avoiding further losses. That was the reason you set the stop-loss at 10%. If you are not convinced your stock will keep dropping after it declines 10%, then set the stop-loss percent a lot lower to avoid frequent selling and buying activities. If the stock increases in value by 10% from the most recent low, I buy it back. For example, it's most recent low was $0.80, a 20% decline from the original price, then I will buy it back at $0.88. This again means that you are convinced the upward trend in your stock price will continue after it gains 10% from its most recent high. I can only tell you that after trying this for a year, I made less money than my soccer moms officemates who simply left their money alone.
- **Dave Ramsey's Investment Strategy** - "The older the better". Pick several mutual funds that have been around

for a long long time, the older the better, preferably over 30 years old that have a good average annual return. Just hold them till retirement.

- **John Bogle's Investment Strategy** - "Buy right, hold tight, stay the course". Allocate your entire portfolio to a broad stock index fund and bond-market fund. Then just watch your money grow.
- **J.L. Collins' Investment Strategy** – "Buy and hold". Put all your money, 90% into VTSAX and 10% into VBTLX and just hold them. According to him, "the market always goes up" based on his 114 year chart. Never mind if their values drop 50% during a bear market in the middle of a recession. He has no exit strategy. His strategy is "buy and hold". Collins is relying on VTSAX's 40 year annual return of 11.9%. He goes through great length in explaining what an 11.9% 40-year average annual return really means. It is almost painful to read the round-about way he seems to tell investors that he does not believe they will ever make 11.9% annual return on their money in the next many years.
- **Joel Greenblatt's Magic Formula Investing Strategy** – Buy undervalued stocks by determining the intrinsic value of companies. Use "earnings yield" (EBIT/Enterprise Value) rather than Price-Earnings Ratio (P/E Ratio). Invest only in companies that have a minimum capitalization of greater than $100 million. Exclude utility and financial stocks. Exclude foreign companies. Once you have chosen the companies, keep buying shares and rebalance your portfolio once a year. This is too much work and too much stress for the average investor, even for someone like me whose job is to create charts and

mathematical models of business and economic statistics and forecasts of market trends, monetary and fiscal policy.
- **Gambling Man's Buy Low Sell High Timing Strategy** – If you are a gambler and do not mind going through some type of stress, this strategy may be for you. We already know that historically, during a period of expansion, the stock market goes through a 10% correction every 12 months or so, and through a 20% correction every 12 to 18 months, you can gamble and time the market by doing this: 1) Start by keeping track of your portfolio balance whenever you want to start. 2) When the Dow goes up 10% from your start date, sell your stocks and put your money into a money market fund (cash equivalents). 3) When the Dow goes down 10% from the date you sold your stocks, put your money back into the same mutual funds they were in before. 4) Repeat the process. The chart below shows a clearer picture of this strategy:

BUY LOW SELL HIGH STRATEGY:				
DATE	DOW	Change	% Change	
Jan 02, 2014	16,441			START DATE
Feb 20, 2015	18,140	1,699	10.33%	SELL
Aug 24, 2015	15,871	-2,269	-12.51%	BUY
Oct 22, 2015	17,489	1,618	10.19%	SELL
Feb 11, 2016	15,660	-1,829	-10.46%	BUY
Mar 14, 2016	17,229	1,569	10.02%	SELL

The chart shows the timeline of the start, buy and sell dates. Theoretically, you will never lose a penny of your principal with this strategy because you will be locking in your gains and the upside profit potential is great. There is a good chance you will out-perform the market. However, there is a downside to every investment strategy, the first one in this case being that this strategy requires nerves of steel. You will have to monitor and keep a chart of DJIA averages daily and prepare to move your money whenever there is a 10% up or down movement. Also, if most of your money is in mutual funds that are "tech heavy", perhaps the NASDAQ averages are what you have to monitor and chart. Finally, you will note that on the preceding chart, the fictitious investor following this investment strategy started charting on Jan 2, 2014 and has made a huge profit since then but has been out of the market since March 14, 2016, waiting for a correction of 10% from his own designated high of 17,229. With this strategy, this means the investor will not go back into the stock market until the Dow goes down to 15,506. This can be a nerve-racking experience. The DJIA averages reached an all-time high in August 2016. The Dow averages may not go back down to 15,506 until the next recession.

Another variation of this strategy is the modified buy low sell high strategy as shown on the chart below. In this strategy the investor will buy whenever the Dow loses 10% but will sell only when the Dow gains 15% so as to compensate for new highs. See the following chart:

MODIFIED BUY LOW SELL HIGH STRATEGY:				
DATE	DOW	Change	% Change	
Jan 02, 2014	16,441			START DATE
Feb 20, 2015	18,140	1,699	10.33%	SELL
Aug 24, 2015	15,871	(2,269)	-12.51%	BUY
Jul 12, 2016	18,348	2,477	15.61%	SELL
???	16,513	(1,835)	-10.00%	BUY
???	18,990	2,477	15.00%	SELL
???	17,091	(1,899)	-10.00%	BUY
???	19,655	2,564	15.00%	SELL

You will note that after the starting date, the investor sold after the Dow gained 10%; bought after the Dow lost 10%; sold after the Dow gained 15%; and will buy when the Dow loses 10% and closes at 16,513; and will sell when the Dow gains 15% and closes at 18,990 and so on as illustrated on the above chart. In this strategy, the investor must compensate for new highs and new lows. If the market consistently breaches resistance and support levels, the investor must adjust by redefining the new resistance and support levels in his chart. Many stock brokers make a lot of money, 20% APY or more on the spread following some type of "buy low-sell high timing strategy".

    Due to my "no stress" game of life strategy, to avoid stress as much as possible, I still prefer my stress-free KISS Principle and Auto-Pilot strategy. I want to sleep like a baby. For those of you who thrive on stress and like gambling a little bit, this strategy may be for you. Feel free to give it a try and let me know how you make out but don't blame me for your losses, if any.

- **Being an Absentee Landlord -** Do not make the same mistake I made. Although being an absentee landlord sounds very appealing to many people and seems like a good idea for investing your money, it is not as easy as it seems. I had money I did not know what to do with in the late eighties so I bought a total of 8 rental townhouses one at a time in a period of 3 years. I got caught up in the rental real estate craze. Although I never had a problem with 90% of my tenants, the remaining 10% bad apples aged me quite a bit. I am sure no rational individual likes dealing with midnight calls about leaky faucets, smell of gas, broken refrigerators, pest infestations, clogged toilets, etc. etc. etc. But this is what you will be dealing with if you become a landlord. It is more work than you think. You prepare and negotiate leases, prep the property after a tenant moves out, check an applicant's credit record, collect the rent, evict tenant if tenant stops paying, spend money for necessary repairs, etc. etc. etc. The numbers do not lie. If I had only dumped my extra cash into my POG, i.e. my retirement accounts instead of supporting the flat and negative cash flows of my rental properties, I would have been ahead by over $500,000.

Crockpot method of investing………..

When it comes to investing in the market, I prefer the crockpot method to the microwave method. I prefer putting all the ingredients in a slow cooker and come home to a nourishing, delicious meal at the end of the day. I have a long-term gain outlook. If you shove a piece of meat in the microwave in order to get a quick meal, you may end up with a partially cooked or a partially burnt meal. In summary, no prophet can predict when the next man-made or natural disaster will occur. Economists and financial analysts cannot accurately time market slowdowns and recessions. Most of them rely on economic data that is outdated as soon as it becomes available. Watching the yield curve is your best chance of timing the market. If you fail to follow my timing strategy and you suddenly find your portfolio has gone down more than 30%, you will be better off to leave your money alone until it recovers in the next bull market. The downward spiral of a bear market during a recession can be quite rapid. The Dow may lose 20% in just the first 10 days of a bear market then may flip-flop between gains and losses for months until it reaches the bottom. Conversely, stocks may gain 20% in just the first 10 days of a post- recession bull market.

Chance Gardener, the idiot character of Peter Sellers in the movie "Being There" would do just as well in economic forecasting as most economists. Note his simple brand of wisdom: ***"In the garden, growth has its seasons. First comes spring and summer, but then we have fall and winter. And then we get spring and summer again. Yes! There will be growth in the spring! As long as the roots are not severed, all is well, and all will be well in the garden."***

Lie #2 – Diversification is good……….

Many financial planners and investment advisors are so hung up on "diversification" that they do it excessively and cannot really justify just why diversification is better. They will tell you, "don't put all your eggs in one basket", "spread the risk", etc. Many of them go to extremes to show the investor their money is safer when allocated across the board among all asset classes in existence. For example, perhaps to justify their fee, many investment advisors go out of their way to show clients that their money is invested in all sectors such as agriculture, mining, utilities, airlines, hotels, construction, insurance, real estate, manufacturing, transportation, finance, banking, health care and many others. In addition, many financial planners further diversify allocation of their clients' holdings into international stocks, developing markets, precious metals, collectibles, treasuries, bonds and money market funds. When the economy goes into a recession and the client loses 50% of his savings and asks, "I thought my money is safe due to diversification?" The investment advisor usually replies, "You did not lose as much as other people..." which in essence is a BS answer. In the first place, you were not making as much as other people who have all their assets in stocks and are not excessively diversified. The worst "diversification" is dividing your holdings between stocks, bonds and money market funds. Bonds and money market funds are earning almost nothing in this era of low interest rates. The truth is, no amount of diversification will protect your savings from cyclical downturns and diminution of assets when the economy goes into a recession. Diversification by putting a portion of your savings into treasuries, bonds and a stable fund (money market) will dilute your returns which will result in lower overall returns. In fact, stocks and bonds go the opposite direction when it comes to return on investment. If you are exposed to many different sectors of the economy, some sectors may react the opposite of others in which case a good return on one investment may be offset by a bad return on another. I have always been heavily invested in stocks, allocated as shown in the next chapter. I have very little in bonds and nothing in cash value. In general, if you are a long term investor, i.e. if you can leave your money alone for 10 years or more, putting all your eggs in one basket should not really hurt you. Take the last recession as an example. Some of the funds that lost the most in 2008 were the Developing Market Funds (Emerging Markets). But they were the best performer during the bull market that followed and most investors who stayed put, in the same funds, recovered their losses in less than two years. Those who moved what remained of their assets to a stable fund, bond fund and large cap fund took many years to recover the losses.

Investment Strategy - Asset Allocation..........

Just to review, the money I have designated as my SF, will be in a lockbox invested in a couple of mutual funds as shown in chapter, **"How I Earned 12% APY".** For the money I will be adding into my POG, I prefer my portfolio to be self-directed. Paying a financial planner 2% to 3% for something I can do just as well is a waste of money. A 401k account has a limited number of funds in a plan but there are many more choices with an IRA at a bank or brokerage. If I have an IRA account I will invest my money in a group of funds through E*Trade, Scottrade or TD Ameritrade following my own strategy defined in the next chapter. At least with these discount brokers you do not have to pay an extra 2% to 3% investment broker/banker fee. You will still pay the mutual fund fees which are interwoven within the funds themselves but you will not pay extra for the "expertise" of a financial planner.

Here is the summary of my investment strategy:

- I try to maximize my contribution to my 401k account, which in 2016 is $18,000. I am dollar-cost-averaging into the stock market with my periodic contributions from every paycheck.

- I have my money in mutual funds not individual stocks. I have a moderately aggressive risk tolerance which means if I lost 50% of my money, I will not panic and withdraw the depreciated balance. I will ride the tide and wait it out until the stock market recovers which it inevitably does. I am more than 10 years away from retirement so I prefer to allocate my assets, 1/8 of my balance into each of these categories of highly rated mutual funds: 1) Large-Cap Growth, 2) Large-Cap Value, 3) Mid-Cap Growth, 4) Mid-Cap Value, 5) Small-Cap Growth, 6) Small-Cap

Value, 7) Balanced and 8) Bonds (Government or AA and AAA only). I selected each category from the following family of funds: Vanguard, T. Rowe Price, Fidelity, Transamerica, John Hancock, Janus, Oppenheimer, Hartford, Invesco, Dreyfus, BlackRock, Janus, Franklin Templeton, Eaton Vance and American Century. The following website shows the best long-term performers in some of the most popular mutual fund categories:

http://money.usnews.com/funds.

Example of Allocation
$500,000 Portfolio, $62,500 in each of these funds:
Large Growth
Vanguard PRIMECAP Fund Adm (VPMAX)

Large Value
American Funds Mutual Fund R6 (RMFGX)

Mid-Cap Growth
Janus Enterprise N (JDMNX)

Mid-Cap Value
American Century NT MdCap Val Instl (ACLMX)

Small Cap Growth
Janus Triton Fund D (JANIX)

Small Cap Value
Vanguard Small-Cap Value Index Fd (VISVX)

Balanced Fund
American Funds American Balanced Fund A (ABALX)

Bond Fund
Vanguard LT Govt Bond Index Inst (VLGIX)

Funds' ratings may be obtained from the Morningstar.com website. Please be aware that the above allocation is only an example. The funds shown above are not specifically recommended. A current fund's performance may be drastically different from its performance on the date of publication of this book. Do your due diligence before acting on any information obtained from this book.

- I automatically rebalance my portfolio at the end of each quarter.

"For everyone who has will be given more, and he will have an abundance. But the one who does not have, even what he has will be taken away from him." The Parable of the Talents, Matthew 25:14-30

PART IV – I AM 5 OR 10 YEARS FROM RETIREMENT, IS IT TOO LATE FOR ME?..........

Retiring within 10 years..........

It is never too late to save for retirement if you have the resources. You should continue dumping as much money as you can afford into that POG. If I think I will need my money within 10 years, I will reduce volatility by moving the amount I would have invested in Small-Cap funds into high quality short term and long term bond funds, AA or AAA rated only. I will stay away from the so-called high yield bond funds. They probably include lots of junk bonds in their portfolio. My asset allocation will be re-adjusted to 62.5% stocks, 37.5% bonds.

Retiring within 5 years……….

If I am retiring within 5 years and think that I may need some of my principal within that time, I would get out of equities all together. The market may be against me when I need to take out some of the money. So I will divide the balance of my portfolio into several high quality bond funds (government, corporate and municipal) with ratings of AA and AAA only. Although there is less volatility in bond funds than equity funds, the bond fund values will still go down during the bear market that follows a recession. Perhaps not by 50% like stocks usually do but by 20% to 30%. If I do not think I will need to take out any money at all within 5 years, i.e. I can leave my portfolio alone for 5 years, then I will invest the full amount as outlined under Chapter, **"Investing in Retirement"**.

Lie #3 - Biggest lie of all – You will pay $400k in taxes on your $1 million savings……….

Every Saturday mornings I hear a New York based financial radio talk show host tell callers, "Be prepared to pay 40% tax on your one million dollar retirement savings…" This of course is a big lie. First of all, under what conditions will make a person withdraw one million dollars of his savings in one year, and declare the full amount as earned income in a single year? None that I can think of. Second, the talk show host should at the very least know that our present tax system is progressive as shown on the following table:

https://www.irs.com/articles/projected-us-tax-rates-2016

SINGLE TAXPAYER

Taxable Income	Tax Rate
$0—$9,275	10%
$9,276—$37,650	$927.50 plus 15% of the amount over $9,275
$37,651—$91,150	$5,183.75 plus 25% of the amount over $37,650
$91,151—$190,150	$18,558.75 plus 28% of the amount over $91,150
$190,151—$ 413,350	$46,278.75 plus 33% of the amount over $190,150
$413,351—$415,050	$119,934.75 plus 35% of the amount over $413,350
$415,051 or more	$120,529.75 plus 39.6% of the amount over $415,050

In accordance with the above IRS chart, you will only pay the highest rate of 39.6% on that portion of your income that exceeds $415,050 (for tax year 2016). Single taxpayers who have reached full retirement age and have saved 1 to 3 million dollars will typically withdraw only 4% ($40,000) or the required minimum distribution (RMD) of their savings so as not to outlive those savings. Finally, even if the talk show host is including New York state and local taxes which are hefty, total tax on an annual retirement income of $40,000 would still not amount to 40%. For more detailed information on why taxes should not worry you, read the Chapter, *"Don't Focus on Taxes"* in the book, **"6m$Retiree"**.

https://www.amazon.com/Six-Million-Dollar-Retiree-retirement-ebook/dp/B073XTL47J/ref=sr_1_4/140-7026794-9692061?s=digital-text&ie=UTF8&qid=1516823179&sr=1-4&keywords=Arthur V. Prosper

UPDATE *The passage of the tax reform bill now officially known as The Tax Cuts and Jobs Act of 2017, Public Law No. 115-97, in which the tax brackets were changed reducing the tax burden of most individual taxpayer only proves that tax consideration should never lord it over a sound investment strategy. Future tax burden is unknowable. You should not plan your investment and retirement strategy based on the current enacted tax law. The pendulum swings the other way about every eight years depending on which party is in power. These lower tax rates will expire in 2025 unless renewed by the incoming 2026 officials of the legislative and executive branches. It may or may not happen. The investment strategy in this book will prove to be sound no matter what the tax system is. For more information, also see Chapter, "How does the new tax law affect the investment strategies in this book?"*

Investing in retirement & required minimum distribution (RMD)..........

I am confident that I will reach my goal in retirement, of having a fully paid house and having enough money to last me well into my 90s if I live that long. When that day comes, I will do a lot of fishing. I do not want to spend much time worrying how my retirement savings is doing today. I want my biggest worry to be figuring out how much money I should donate to charities this week, what kind of fish to catch today, how to cook my catch and what type of wine goes well with my catch. So as soon as I stop working, I will re-allocate my assets this way, 40% in a Large-Cap value fund, 40% in a Mid-Cap value fund, 20% in a government Bond Fund. I will re-balance my portfolio each quarter. I will limit my withdrawals to 4% per annum or the RMD whichever is lower. I will take my withdrawals from the Bond Fund. I will continue to monitor the stock market and make necessary adjustments according to my system.

Note that there is a strict rule on RMDs. Penalty is severe, a whopping 50% on the required undistributed amount. You must take the RMD by April 1 of the year following the year you turned 70 ½. Open these IRS links for more information,

https://www.irs.gov/pub/irs-tege/uniform_rmd_wksht.pdf

https://www.irs.gov/publications/p590b/ch01.html#en_US_2016_publink1000230772

https://www.irs.gov/retirement-plans/plan-participant-employee/required-minimum-distribution-worksheets

The IRS links above will take you to a worksheet to figure out your RMD. If you are still working at age 70 1/2, you don't have to take RMDs from your current employer's 401k plan until you leave your job. This is the "still working exception". To qualify for this exception, you must be considered employed throughout the entire year, own no more than 5% of the company and your 401k plan allows you to delay RMDs. For this reason, it is a good idea to transfer all of your other taxable retirement accounts, traditional 401k and IRAs to your current employer's plan if your plan accepts rollovers so as to avoid the annual RMD if you don't need to take any of the money out. However, if you are already 70 ½, you must first take the RMD from your IRA before rolling the balance over to your company's 401k plan.

RMD rules are complex and the rules often change. The explanations in the IRS website will confuse the average tax payer. A seasoned accountant, retirement planner or tax professional can simplify the rules and customize an RMD plan for you but here is the general idea behind the RMD rules. If your spouse is the sole beneficiary of your IRA or 401k, he or she will inherit your plan and the same rules will apply as if it's his or hers. For unmarried owners of the plan and married owners whose spouses are not more than 10 years younger, and owners whose spouses are not the sole beneficiaries of their plan, the following distribution table applies:

Unmarried Owners, Married Owners Whose Spouse Are Not More Than 10 Years Younger, and Married Owners Whose Spouses Are Not the Sole Beneficiaries of Their IRAs)

Age	Distribution Period	Age	Distribution Period
70	27.4	93	9.6
71	26.5	94	9.1
72	25.6	95	8.6
73	24.7	96	8.1
74	23.8	97	7.6
75	22.9	98	7.1
76	22	99	6.7
77	21.2	100	6.3
78	20.3	101	5.9
79	19.5	102	5.5
80	18.7	103	5.2
81	17.9	104	4.9
82	17.1	105	4.5
83	16.3	106	4.2
84	15.5	107	3.9
85	14.8	108	3.7
86	14.1	109	3.4
87	13.4	110	3.1
88	12.7	111	2.9
89	12	112	2.6
90	11.4	113	2.4
91	10.8	114	2.1
92	10.2	115 and over	1.9

According to the preceding table, if you were 70 ½ years old by the end of the year, and your plan balance is $1,000,000 your RMD is $36,496.35 (balance divided by life expectancy). You must take this distribution by April 1 of the following year but you should take it before year end so you won't get stuck with 2 RMDs the following year which may put you in a higher tax bracket.

The rules are more complicated for plan owners whose spouses are more than 10 years younger and are the sole beneficiaries of their spouse's plan. In the wisdom of our legislators who have hundreds of actuaries, tax experts and economists working for them all day long, they came up with a system for RMD based on "Joint Life and Last Survivor Expectancy". They devised RMD Table II (Table) to come up with a "blended" life expectancy for the owner and survivor. The rationale behind this is that the government does not want to wait too long to collect taxes on the older spouse's plan. The website below is an excellent resource for figuring out your RMD. Just enter the required information and click "calculate". A report will show up on the screen and you can print a PDF report of the table.

https://www.calcxml.com/calculators/qua07;jsessionid=F658D4F9462B62CA072EAEC8D35DDDCE?skn=#

If you have retired and are one of the lucky top 10% who have more than a million dollars in your retirement accounts, take at least the annual RMD and pay the taxes. You should not outlive your money if it is invested the way I have outlined in this book and if you do not sustain catastrophic losses whenever the market crashes.

If you need more money, take more than the RMD. If your money earns at least 4% APR you will be taking out approximately $40,000 to $65,000 a year until you are over 100 years old. Pay the tax each year. It would not be so bad. Don't be too greedy. You have successfully used the tax system to your advantage, why not pay your due now? Most people have less income in retirement than when they were working. If you're the opposite, be glad, thank God and pay the taxes. Follow the taxation advice in the book, **"*6m$Retiree*"**. If you maximize your deferral and take advantage of all the legal tax deductions, you will have paid much less in taxes by the time you retire than others who will not follow my advice. Some financial advisors recommend buying a QLAC (Qualified Longevity Annuity Contract) at this point to defer RMD and tax payment, but I would not recommend them. Take the RMD and pay the taxes annually now at this point in your life rather than defer the taxes until you are 85 years old. If you have dependents depending on you for financial support, pay some of their expenses from the after-tax money. Check with your tax accountant if you may be able to claim any of them as dependents (qualifying relatives) on your tax return so as to reduce your taxes. Better still, if you have too much money, give a big portion of it to charity to reduce your taxes or just invest the after tax money. Some financial advisors recommend buying a life insurance policy with the RMD if you don't need any of the money to live on. That way you can leave tax free money (insurance death benefit proceeds) to your beneficiaries. But is this really more advantageous than just leaving taxable inheritance to your heirs? Find out in the book, **"*6m$Retiree*"**. If you are adamant about minimizing taxes in retirement, another option that many finance gurus (aka "Financial Entertainers") advocate is to start a foundation so as to reduce your taxes. Click on the link below to learn more:

http://www.thebusinessofgood.org/get-engaged/starting-a-foundation.aspx

According to these finance gurus you may be able to deduct many business expenses (*wink wink*) from your tax returns if you have a foundation. Examples of these "business expenses" are: vacations, cruises, casino trips, cars, yachts, gardening, janitorial services and many other expenses. In a recent guest appearance on WOR radio, a NYC based station, **Bill Bresnan**, who was a popular radio talk show host in the 1990s, said you can use your yacht or go on a cruise and deduct the expenses from your taxes if your trips were related to your charitable work. He gave examples such as, attending a party in Paris, investigating wildlife in the Galapagos or touring Costa Rica to observe the bird population in the wilderness so you can decide if it is worth it to donate money to the Audubon Society. He concluded by saying, "The IRS does not like it but there is nothing they can do until Congress changes the tax system. You are not breaking the law". As for me, do I really want to get involved in any of this in my old age? If I have 2 million dollars at the age of 70, with my lifestyle, I will never spend it all in my lifetime. And how much money to leave my children is really not that important to me nor to them. So all I want to plan for today, tomorrow and the following day is, "where am I going fishing?" I also want to plan a trip every couple of months to every exotic location in the world I can think of. Right now I am thinking of Bora Bora, Bhutan, Myanmar, Galapagos, Maldives, Alice Springs, Victoria Falls, Machu Picchu, Cape Town and hundreds of other tourist spots on my bucket list. Geeeeeez, I can't wait!

Other investments before and during retirement……….

100% in Bonds - If your risk tolerance is a lot lower than mine, i.e. if a 10% to 50% drop in the stock market will drive you crazy, then put your entire portfolio into 4 different bond funds that are rated AA+. Avoid a fund that has junk bonds in it. Select funds that have a "below average risk" rating. You will not receive a return of 13% to 20% APR during bull markets as you would in Small Caps or Emerging market equity funds, but in the long run, you will average just slightly lower. Best of all, you can put your money in and forget it.

Annuities, what are they?..........

Car leases and annuities are the most mysterious deals most people will ever encounter. In my experience with both products, the salesperson employs diversionary tactics and mumbo jumbo to convince you that you are getting a good deal. He will avoid telling you the equivalent effective annual interest rate you will be paying in case of an auto lease or that you will be receiving in case of an annuity. Instead, the salesperson will divert your attention towards the monthly payments you will be paying or receiving and other benefits and advantages these product may have over others. Annuity salesmen will neatly hide the deficiencies of these products within the very fine print of the contract that you will need a lawyer to review it and to tell you that what you are getting is a bad deal. That is the reason I have included this chapter in this book.

Think of annuities as "reverse-insurance". With an insurance policy, the sooner you die, the better it is financially speaking to your beneficiaries. You will pay less in premiums and your beneficiaries will immediately receive the tax-free death benefit. With an annuity, you either give the insurance company a lump sum or fund the annuity account with regular payments for a promise of a guaranteed income for a definite period of time or for as long as you live. The longer you live, the more money the insurance company will pay out. Some annuity contracts have long term care clauses and some of them have death benefit options.

I have concluded that annuities are not for me. I am looking for growth of my investments and I am willing to take the risk following my own system of saving and investing for a high return. But for people who are looking for preservation of capital, not growth, guaranteed return and do not mind turning over a big portion of their lifetime savings in one lump sum to an insurance company or fund an annuity contract (accumulation phase) for a period of time in return for a promise of principal protection, guaranteed income and perhaps to take care of the cost of long term care, annuities may be for you. The following information came from the U.S. Securities and Exchange Commission:

An annuity is a contract between you and an insurance company that requires the insurer to make payments to you, either immediately or in the future. You buy an annuity by making either a single payment or a series of payments. Similarly, your payout may come either as one lump-sum payment or as a series of payments over time.

People typically buy annuities to help manage their income in retirement. Annuities provide three things:

- Periodic payments for a specific amount of time. This may be for the rest of your life, or the life of your spouse or another person.

- Death benefits. If you die before receiving payments, the person you name as your beneficiary receives a specific payment.

- Tax-deferred growth. You pay no taxes on the income and investment gains from your annuity until you withdraw the money.

There are three basic types of annuities, fixed, variable and indexed. Here is how they work:

- Fixed annuity. The insurance company promises you a minimum rate of interest and a fixed amount of periodic payments. Fixed annuities are regulated by state insurance commissioners. Please check with your <u>state insurance commission</u> about the risks and benefits of fixed annuities and to confirm that your insurance broker is registered to sell insurance in your state.

- Variable annuity. The insurance company allows you to direct your annuity payments to different investment options, usually mutual funds. Your payout will vary depending on how much you put in, the rate of return on your investments, and expenses. The SEC regulates variable annuities.

- Indexed annuity. This annuity combines features of securities and insurance products. The insurance company credits you with a return that is based on a stock market index, such as the Standard & Poor's 500 Index. Indexed annuities are regulated by the state insurance commissioners.

Some people look to annuities to "insure" their retirement and to receive periodic payments once they no longer receive a salary. There are two phases to annuities, the accumulation phase and the payout phase.

- During the accumulation phase, you make payments that may be split among various investment options. In addition, variable annuities often allow you to put some of your money in an account that pays a fixed rate of interest.

- During the payout phase, you get your payments back, along with any investment income and gains. You may take the payout in one lump-sum payment, or you may choose to receive a regular stream of payments, generally monthly.

All investments carry a level of risk. Make sure you consider the financial strength of the insurance company issuing the annuity. You want to be sure the company will still be around, and financially sound, during your payout phase.

Variable annuities have a number of features that you need to understand before you invest. Understand that variable annuities are designed as an investment for long-term goals, such as retirement. They are not suitable for short-term goals because you typically will pay substantial taxes and charges or other penalties if you withdraw your money early. Variable annuities also involve investment risks, just as mutual funds do.

Insurance companies sell annuities, as do some banks, brokerage firms, and mutual fund companies. Make sure you read and understand your annuity contract. All fees should be clearly stated in the contract. Your most important source of information about investment options within a variable annuity is the mutual fund prospectus. Request prospectuses for all the mutual fund options you might want to select. Read the prospectuses carefully before you decide how to allocate your purchase payments among the investment options.

Realize that if you are investing in a variable annuity through a tax-advantaged retirement plan, such as a 401(k) plan or an Individual Retirement Account, you will get no additional tax advantages from a variable annuity. In such cases, consider buying a variable annuity only if it makes sense because of the annuity's other features.

Note that if you sell or withdraw money from a variable annuity too soon after your purchase, the insurance company will impose a "surrender charge." This is a type of sales charge that applies in the "surrender period," typically six to eight years after you buy the annuity. Surrender charges will reduce the value of -- and the return on -- your investment.

You will pay several charges when you invest in a variable annuity. Be sure you understand all charges before you invest. Besides surrender charges, there are a number of other charges, including:

- Mortality and expense risk charge. This charge is equal to a certain percentage of your account value, typically about 1.25% per year. This charge pays the issuer for the insurance risk it assumes under the annuity contract. The profit from this charge sometimes is used to pay a commission to the person who sold you the annuity.

- Administrative fees. The issuer may charge you for record keeping and other administrative expenses. This may be a flat annual fee, or a percentage of your account value.

- Underlying fund expenses. In addition to fees charged by the issuer, you will pay the fees and expenses for underlying mutual fund investments.

- Fees and charges for other features. Additional fees typically apply for special features, such as a guaranteed minimum income benefit or long-term care insurance. Initial sales loads, fees for transferring part of your account from one investment option to another, and other fees also may apply.

- Penalties. If you withdraw money from an annuity before you are age 59 ½, you may have to pay a 10% tax penalty to the Internal Revenue Service on top of any taxes you owe on the income.

Variable annuities are considered to be securities. All broker-dealers and investment advisers that sell variable annuities must be registered. Before buying an annuity from a broker or adviser, confirm that they are registered <u>using BrokerCheck</u> and click on this website, **FINRA's BrokerCheck website**.

In most cases, the investments offered within a variable annuity are mutual funds. By law, each mutual fund is required to file a prospectus and regular shareholder reports with the SEC. Before you invest, be sure to read these materials.

If the preceding article from the SEC does not yet discourage you on buying annuities, read on. Fixed and Indexed annuities are in essence insurance contracts. Most of them are sold by insurance companies such as Allstate, Fidelity Insurance, John Hancock, Met Life, AXA, Prudential and others. Variable annuities are in essence insured investments in mutual funds and are generally sold by brokerage firms. Annuities are not guaranteed by the government. Your money will disappear if the annuity provider disappears. The most common slogan of annuity salesmen is: "You make money when the stock market goes up, but you won't lose money when the stock market goes down". They insure the APY on fixed and indexed annuities and you pay a premium for that guaranteed return. The annual expenses can be as much as 3% a year. Example, if an annuity is indexed to the S&P 500 which averaged 10% in one year, your annuity will earn a return of 7% that year. On the other hand, you are protected on the down side and your annuity will still earn a minimum return even in a year when the S&P 500 had a negative yield. I prefer my own investment and allocation of asset strategy.

Before signing a contract, make sure to read the fine print. Better still, in your first meeting with the broker, request a prospectus that you can take home with you. It is important to ask about principal protection (insurance), annual fees on fixed and variable, long term care rider, investment options, death benefits and annuity payout options.

If you still think that an annuity may be right for you, the website below is an excellent source for additional information for fixed annuities.

https://www.immediateannuities.com/information/annuity-rates-step-1.html

Enter the lump sum amount you want to annuitize today. Enter your age and other pertinent information. Various offers of monthly payouts will pop up for the amount you want to annuitize. If you click on the (?) the terms are explained in plain non-legalese language. The payout amounts shown represent interest and return of principal. After the page with your information pops up, you will notice that there are different pay outs and types of coverages such as "Joint Life", "Single Life" and "Period Certain" options, e.g. for life, 25, 20, 15, 10 and 5 years. After I entered information for a person who just reached full retirement age (FRA) which at the time of writing is age 66, has $300,000 to invest and wants a monthly payout for a 10-year period certain, with no cost of living increase, I received a best offer of $2,780 monthly payment. This annuity payout represents a 2.18% annual percent return on the money. You may confirm the rate of return by clicking on the website below. Enter the initial principal amount = $300,000 and monthly withdrawal = $2780.00 annuitized over 10 years, then click calculate to see the annual growth rate.

http://www.bankrate.com/calculators/investing/annuity-calculator.aspx

My opinion is that I can do a lot better than a 2.18% APR by investing on my own.

 The payouts include principal and interest, so the interest portion of the annuity is taxable as ordinary income. Click on this IRS website for information on how the interest is calculated, https://www.irs.gov/taxtopics/tc411.html

"Wealth consists not in having great possessions, but in having few wants."

- Epictetus

The $50,000 question: What if I don't have $50,000?

For starters, read the book, "***"Dynamic Budgeting Techniques" ("DynBudgTech"),***

https://www.amazon.com/Dynamic-Budgeting-Techniques-expenses-double-ebook/dp/B01LZA9O3W/ref=sr_1_7?s=digital-text&ie=UTF8&qid=1506100005&sr=1-7&keywords=Arthur V. Prosper

This book will show you how to control your finances, create a cash flow statement and devise a budget plan so that you will always have money left over every month which should expedite the process of saving $50,000.

Many people don't have this amount of savings at 30 years old, but many people do. My wife and I had $100,000 cash in the bank at age 30 which we did not know what to do with. The basic premise in this book is to put aside the $50,000 as your SF, not to co-mingle it with other savings, lock it away for 37 years and watch that money grow into $3.3 million. If you don't have this much money to put aside, put aside as much as you can targeted for this investment program. You don't even have to add new money to the principal amount of $50,000 once you reach this target, but you cannot touch this money at all if you have a choice. Not for payment of debts, new purchases, insurance premiums, college costs or down payment on a house. This specific money is not for any of those purposes. Of course if you have no choice and really need the money, there is nothing you can do but to dip into it. But you really have to think hard to see if you can obtain the money you need elsewhere, from other sources. If you do not have this amount of money yet, you can start your SF with what you have but take the following steps as soon as possible:

- Review your cash flow and develop a budget, as shown in the book, **"DynBudgTech"**, so that you will always have a surplus at month-end that you can then add to your SF so you can build it up to $50,000. Keep adding the surplus to your IRA/401k retirement savings as a fast track to starting this investment program. There are many ideas in the book, **"DynBudgTech"** on how to increase your income and reduce your expenses. When you start the cash flow worksheet from the book, you will know exactly where every dollar is spent and where you need to cut back.

- Get rid of all your non-mortgage debts or ask your creditors for reduction or forgiveness of those debts. The interest you are paying on consumer loans, i.e. credit cards, department stores, car loans, home improvement loans, etc. will eat away at the money that you need to start this investment program. Download the book, ***"Stop Paying Your Credit Cards"*** to explore the possibility of asking your creditors to forgive a big portion of your credit card debt,

https://www.amazon.com/Stop-Paying-Your-Credit-Cards-ebook/dp/B019ZY3D1E/ref=pd_sbs_351_2?_encoding=UTF8&psc=1&refRID=N2WEKMATRVAE5T3Z1TJ3

- If you are worried about the cost of higher education for yourself, your spouse or your children and you think college costs would keep you from saving enough money to start this investment program, download the book, ***"Living Rich and Loving It"***. There are many ideas in the book that if implemented might help increase financial aid offers and reduce the costs of college education.

https://www.amazon.com/Living-Rich-Loving-healthy-balanced-ebook/dp/B01GORIB4Y/ref=asap_bc?ie=UTF8

- The book, **"DynBudgTech"** offers ideas on how to live a simple and frugal life at least until you save your SF of $50,000. My wife and I kept a tight budget. At age 30, we could well afford a brand new $50,000 Mercedes or BMW just like what the yuppies were driving at that time, but we opted for a Toyota Corolla. We opened the windows instead of turning on our air conditioner in the summer months which is a feat in itself if you live in the NYC metro area. We did not go out to restaurants for dinner for five years except to McDonald's and KFC and bought Chinese Take-out. We did not go out to see movies. We rented VHS tapes instead from Blockbuster. We packed lunches for our children in grade school and for ourselves on workdays. We reduced all our insurance costs. We never bought jewelries and clothing that we did not need. We comparison shopped whenever we went grocery shopping and always bought generic brand products. We lived way below our means. That was how we accumulated $100,000 by age 30. Being frugal is nothing to be ashamed of. Many billionaires such as Warren Buffett who still lives in a house he bought in 1958 for $31,500 and Mark Zuckerberg who drives a modest 2014 manual transmission VW hatchback are actually frugal people.

> A spendthrift person is actually someone who lives like a millionaire and in the process never becomes one.
> - Arthur V. Prosper

How does the new tax law affect the investment strategies in this book?

The passage of The tax reform bill into law, now officially known as the Tax Cuts and Jobs Act of 2017 ("TCJA") Public law no. 115-97, only proves my point that we should NOT focus too much on taxes when formulating an investment and retirement strategy. Making long term investment and retirement plans based on taxation is an exercise in futility because future tax rates and other tax changes are unknowable. The pendulum swings the other way every 8 years. The tax cuts in this recently passed TCJA will expire in 2025. If a Democrat wins back the White House and the Democrats take back the House and Senate, it is almost certain the Trump Tax Cuts will be allowed to expire and the tax rates will revert back to the 2017 tax brackets. Moreover, tax increases are likely when Democrats are back in power. That's not a political statement. It's just a fact of life.

There are so many variables in your own personal savings and investment situation and idiosyncrasies in the way you manage your life that I am sure you don't really know how the new tax law will affect you. For this reason, I decided to publish a new book entitled:

How Much Federal Income Tax Will I Pay in 2018?

https://www.amazon.com/Much-Federal-Income-Will-2018-ebook/dp/B078Z5LXGJ/ref=sr_1_1/146-7233552-6714568?s=digital-text&ie=UTF8&qid=1516034997&sr=1-1&keywords=Arthur V. Prosper

This book is only available on Amazon Kindle. The aforementioned book contains comparison charts of how much federal tax you will pay under the current tax system and how much you will pay under the new system. All you have to do is choose the table that closely resembles your income level, filing status and deductions. If none of the charts is applicable to your own unique situation, email **Arthur V. Prosper** for the editable excel tax worksheet. Copy and paste the Program Code below. When you receive the excel worksheet, you can enter your income level and deductions on the spreadsheet. The taxes for 2017 and 2018 will automatically calculate.

Email address: <u>Arthur V. Prosper@Arthur V. Prosper.com</u>

Copy and Paste: **Editable Excel Worksheet Program Code: SPW0702**

Conclusion

Turning $50,000 into $3.3 million should be as easy as reading this book. Time and Yield are the two main components of this investment program. The longer time can work for you, the more money you will end up with. You will be right on target or above the target of an average 12% APY if you follow my investment timing strategy. My timing strategy will always beat the "buy and hold" strategy. I have averaged more than a 12% APY in the last 30 years due to the following reasons: 1) my money is invested in a number of mutual funds as shown under Chapter, **"Investment Strategy – Asset Allocation"** inside my 401k retirement account. 2) I do not buy and sell my shares during dips and rises in the stock market in periods of economic recovery (expansions). I "buy and hold" until an identifiable recession is in sight. 3) I follow my timing system shown in chapter, **"Inverted yield curve, a harbinger of gloom and doom".** I get out of mutual funds before the start of the bear market that follows a recession. 4) I return my money into the same mutual funds before the beginning of the bull market that precedes a recovery.

****

If this book helped you, your positive Amazon review would be much appreciated.

****

If you have questions or comments, VISIT THE AUTHOR'S WEBSITE and click:

http://Arthur V. Prosper.com/contact/

http://Arthur V. Prosper.com/

****

Living Rich & Loving It

Learn more about the subjects below from the author's new book,

> https://www.amazon.com/Living-Rich-Loving-healthy-balanced-ebook/dp/B01GORIB4Y/ref=sr_1_3?s=digital-text&ie=UTF8&qid=1471625403&sr=1-3&keywords=Arthur V. Prosper

- **Find a job you love** – If you cannot wait to get up and get to work every morning, then you have found the job you love. Otherwise, you need to read this chapter and the chapter, "Increase Your Income with these Ideas".

- **Personal Insurance** – Which is better, whole life or term insurance? How much insurance do you need? The answer may surprise you.

- **Budgeting made easy** - Follow the sample and simple budget in the book and you will always have a monthly surplus.

- **Never buy Veblen Goods** – the savings will amaze you.

- **Shop around for everything** – if you are struggling to make ends meet, this chapter will show you why. Learn how to save more and spend less.

- **How to purchase your primary residence** – Pros and cons of owning vs. renting. The analysis chart shows the clear winner which will surprise you.

- Good debt, bad debt – when borrowing makes sense. Analysis table proves that some debts are good.

- Do Not Take Unnecessary Risks, Don't Do Anything Stupid – this chapter shows that stupidity is the great equalizer in life. Doing any of the things on the list may change your life or worse end it in the blink of an eye.

- Never invest in a rental property – this chapter tells you why it is not worth being an absentee landlord.

- Never keep an emergency fund – the analysis chart shows you why and the answer will astound you.

- No Double Taxation on 401k Loans – never ever listen to Suze Orman that 401k loans are taxed twice. They are not and a chapter in the book proves it.

- Planning for College – how to fund your children's college education. Read the many different ideas in this chapter which includes the availability of financial aid packages. The chart shows which colleges to choose and guides you towards a prudent decision.

- Increase Your Income - Make more money in your spare time with these ideas. When you read the money-making ideas in this chapter, you will scratch your head and say, "why didn't I think of that?"

- Create a Document Storage and Retrieval System – So simple yet so effective. It will free up a lot of your limited living space.

- Stress-Free Personal Time Management – This system will organize your day and free up plenty of your time for use at your leisure.

- How to Store and Safeguard Passwords – Simple trick will help you create and remember strong passwords.

- How to maximize your Social Security benefits – In light of the elimination of "File and Suspend" and "Restricted Application" strategies, the chart shows claiming strategies for 1) Single never married, 2) currently married, 3) married at least 10 years, divorced at least 2 years, currently single, 4) divorced, has remarried and currently married, 5) widow/widower, 6) surviving divorced spouse, married at least 10 years, currently single or remarried after the age of 60.

- Best places for retirement – Some of these retirement communities are surprising. Some viable locations have ½ the cost of living of most cities in the U.S. But should you pack your bags and move now? Find out the answer in this book.

- Paying for Nursing Home and Long-Term Care

- How to qualify for Medicaid benefits for LTC
- How to reduce income to qualify for Medicaid

- How to reduce assets to qualify for Medicaid.

- Estate Planning – How to protect your estate from estate tax and inheritance tax.

- o **Enrich Your Life by Exploring the World – Travel as soon as you can while you are still young. This chapter discusses why the money you spend traveling and exploring the world is money well spent.**

- o **Staying Healthy and Fit as You Age – There are a few minor behavior modification changes that you can put into practice that will keep you healthy throughout your retirement years.**

- o **Live a Rich, Happy, Healthy, Simple and Balanced Life**

Excerpt from the book, Living Rich & Loving It:
LIVE A RICH, HAPPY, HEALTHY, SIMPLE AND BALANCED LIFE

Life does not have to be complicated. If you succeed in following the life strategies in this book, your children will end up well, your investments will provide you with a nice retirement nest egg that will last for as long as you live, you will minimize stress in your life and you will have more time for leisure and for activities that help keep your mind and body healthy. This book is not the magic bullet for success but a playbook to improve your odds for achieving success. There will be unexpected twists and turns in your life but the principles and strategies in this book will help lead you to the correct path to success and keep you on track to achieve all you want in life. If you have goals, dreams and aspirations in life, you have a sense of direction but you still need a road map to take you from here to there. I hope this book will serve as that road map for you.

Having a balanced life for me does not only mean having equal portions of work, play and family life. For me, it does not only mean having a sound mind, body and spirit. What I believe is that it is within us to muster the forces of nature to be on our side by reforming our own behavior in order to achieve a well-balanced life. If you do "the right thing", the right thing will come back to you. This is not necessarily karma but the realization that there is positive and negative energy in the universe that is out of our control and beyond our comprehension. Besides gravity and centrifugal force, there are forces in the universe we will never comprehend---frequencies, vibrations, fields of energy, our life force energy that affect people around us. I believe that doing the right thing will harness and call on all these forces to rally behind us. If it won't take too much effort on our part, why not choose to do the right thing? In doing so, I believe we will achieve the unity of mind, body, emotion and spirit which will awaken the genius in us. It is combining the fundamental rules of life with common sense, with the sum of our knowledge and with the unexplainable power of the universe…………

Supplemental Disclaimer

The information contained in this book is provided to you "AS IS" and does not constitute legal or financial advice. All sample forms are for educational purposes only. We make no claims, promises or guarantees about the accuracy, completeness, or any specific result from the use of the contents or adequacy of the information contained in this book. Information contained in this book should not be used as substitute for obtaining financial and tax advice from a competent and licensed financial advisor and/or legal advice from an attorney licensed or authorized to practice in your jurisdiction. Medical or health information written in this book must not be misconstrued as medical advice. Consult your doctor or other healthcare provider before acting on any information provided in this book. Narratives in this book are based on true events.

No warranties are made regarding the suitability of this book. This book contains an accumulation of information based on the personal experience of the author. Prior results do not guarantee a similar outcome. The author and publisher does not guarantee the accuracy, completeness, efficacy and timeliness of the information provided herein. The information may no longer be current at the time of publication of this book. The reader should seek the advice of a licensed professional before acting on any information provided herein.

Various advice in this book do not take into account your objectives, financial situation or needs. Before acting on any advice you should consider the appropriateness of the advice and its applicability to your current situation. Any products mentioned in this book may not be appropriate for you. Product Disclosure Statements for those products must be requested and reviewed before making any decisions. We make no claims, promises or guarantees about the accuracy, completeness, or any specific result from the use of the contents or adequacy of the information contained in this book. **Arthur V. Prosper**, its affiliates, parents, subsidiaries, assigns, officers, directors, shareholders, employees, representatives, agents and servants assume no responsibility to any person who relies on information contained herein and disclaim all liability in respect to such information.

Copyright and Trademark Ownership

Please be aware that any unauthorized use of the contents contained herein violates copyright laws, trademark laws, the laws of privacy and publicity, and/or other regulations and statutes. All text, images and other materials provided herein are owned by **Arthur V. Prosper** unless otherwise attributed to third parties. None of the content on these materials may be copied, reproduced, distributed, downloaded, displayed, or transmitted in any form without the prior written permission of the author, the legal copyright owner. However, you may copy, reproduce, distribute, download, display, or transmit the content of the materials for personal, non-commercial use provided that full attribution and citation to the author, Arthur V. Prosper is included and the content is not modified, and you retain all copyright and other proprietary notices contained in the content. The permission stated above is automatically rescinded if you breach any of these terms or conditions. If permission is rescinded or denied, you must immediately destroy any downloaded and/or printed content.

PUBLISHER: A-TEAM, LP - PUBLISHER'S CATALOG:

DEBT FORGIVENESS Volume 2 WHEN CREDITORS DECIDE TO SUE: Erase Your Credit Card Debts
https://www.amazon.com/DEBT-FORGIVENESS-WHEN-CREDITORS-DECIDE-ebook/dp/B01ACTBTIU/ref=pd_sim_351_1?_encoding=UTF8&pd_rd_i=B01ACTBTIU&pd_rd_r=A001FFR7YYMRE7EEJ7T3&pd_rd_w=lDdkz&pd_rd_wg=W1P4U&psc=1&refRID=A001FFR7YYMRE7EEJ7T3

The Six Million Dollar Retiree: Your roadmap to a six million dollar retirement nest egg
https://www.amazon.com/Six-Million-Dollar-Retiree-retirement-ebook/dp/B073XTL47J/ref=sr_1_4?s=digital-text&ie=UTF8&qid=1504026864&sr=1-4&keywords=Arthur V. Prosper

Dynamic Budgeting Techniques: Cut your expenses in half and double your income
https://www.amazon.com/Dynamic-Budgeting-Techniques-expenses-double-ebook/dp/B01LZA9O3W/ref=asap_bc?ie=UTF8

Living Rich & Loving It: Your guide to a rich, happy, healthy, simple and balanced life
https://www.amazon.com/Living-Rich-Loving-healthy-balanced-ebook/dp/B01GORIB4Y/ref=sr_1_3?s=digital-text&ie=UTF8&qid=1480539481&sr=1-3&keywords=Arthur V. Prosper

Stop Paying Your Credit Cards: Obtain Credit Card Debt Forgiveness Volume 1
https://www.amazon.com/gp/product/B019ZY3D1E/ref=dbs_a_def_rwt_bibl_vppi_i0

Made in the USA
Middletown, DE
26 September 2018